The Japanese Pantry

Alayna Tucker

Photographs by Alayna Tucker
2012

CONTENTS

INTRODUCTION	1
BASICS:	5
DASHI	7
STOVETOP SUSHI RICE	8
SUSHI-SU	9
INGREDIENTS:	11
SUSHI KOME - SHORT GRAIN RICE	12
SHOYU - SOY SAUCE	15
MISO - FERMENTED SOY BEAN PASTE	18
MIRIN - SWEET RICE SEASONING	22
KOMEZU - RICE VINEGAR	25
SAKE - FERMENTED RICE ALCOHOL	28
WASABI - JAPANESE HORSERADISH	31
TOFU - SOY BEAN CURD	35
GOMA - SESAME SEEDS	38

PANKO - JAPANESE BREAD CRUMBS	41
RAMEN - FRIED INSTANT NOODLES	45
SOBA - BUCKWHEAT NOODLES	48
UDON - THICK WHEAT NOODLES	52
NORI - SEAWEED PAPER	55
NEGI - SCALLIONS	59
SHIITAKE - FRAGRANT MUSHROOM	62
EDAMAME - YOUNG SOY BEANS	66
KABOCHA - JAPANESE PUMPKIN	70
DAIKON - JAPANESE RADISH	73
SATSUMA-IMO - JAPANESE SWEET POTATO	77
KURI - CHESTNUT	81
AZUKI - SWEET RED BEAN	85
NASHI - ASIAN PEAR	88
KAKI - PERSIMMON	91
MATCHA - GREEN TEA POWDER	94

武士はくわねど高楊枝

Bushi wa kuwanedo taka youji

Even if a samurai hasn't eaten, he holds his toothpick high.

"Live as if you are feasting, even if you are hungry."

- Japanese Proverb

"So, you make sushi every night?"

That's the typical response when I tell someone new that I cook mostly Japanese food at home.

It's understandable, really. Our Western view into the cuisine of Japan has largely been through that of sushi restaurants, which started gaining popularity in the late 80's and early 90's. Aside from an occasional California Roll on a date or bowl of ramen noodles in college, Westerners just don't get much exposure to what Japanese people really eat.

Of course every meal in Japan isn't just night after night of sushi dinners. The reality is that Japanese people eat a diverse diet rich in fish and other meats, leafy green vegetables and seaweeds, many varieties of rice that play a starring role in dishes rather than supporting, pickled and fermented products, and occasional fruits – usually eaten as a healthy dessert.

Japanese food, on the whole, is far more comforting and homey than those artful and intricately-crafted rolls of sushi would lead you to believe. There is certainly a care and attention to detail that exists across Japanese cooking, but it doesn't have to be fussy or complicated. It certainly isn't in my kitchen, and I've been careful not to include any recipes in this book that require any kind of expert skill or special knowledge to execute.

In fact, this isn't really a Japanese cookbook at all.

"Wait, what?"

I am by no means an expert on traditional Japanese cooking, but I have incorporated many Japanese ingredients into my pantry and made them staples in my household. You won't find steak sauce in my refrigerator, but you will find teriyaki sauce. More adventurous cooks may keep a bottle of wine around for cooking; I keep a bottle of sake. What I hope to show you in this book is how you can incorporate new ingredients into your own pantry without necessarily having to make any changes to the way you already cook or learn an entirely new cuisine.

You may be surprised to find that you already keep some of these ingredients on hand. I've taken much care to list only ingredients that I've been able to find in regular grocery stores or in gourmet markets such as Whole Foods. If your town doesn't have a bustling Asian grocer of it's own, no problem!

The recipes in this book will show you how you can put these ingredients to use. Some are my shortcuts to creating a traditional Japanese dish with fewer ingredients and less fuss. Some are twists on familiar Western classics utilizing a Japanese ingredient to lend an unexpected punch of flavor. And still others are totally new recipes of my own creation.

My hope is that the recipes in this book will help to familiarize you with the everyday Japanese ingredients that are available to you so that they may feel less exotic and more exciting. There is no need to feel intimidated by a new ingredient. It's all just food, though maybe not a food you've dared to try before. I challenge you to incorporate some of the ingredients herein into your own cooking and see which ones become part of your Japanese pantry.

腹が減っては戦ができぬ

Hara ga hette wa ikusa ga dekinu

An army marches on its stomach.

"You can't fight a battle on an empty stomach."

- Japanese Proverb

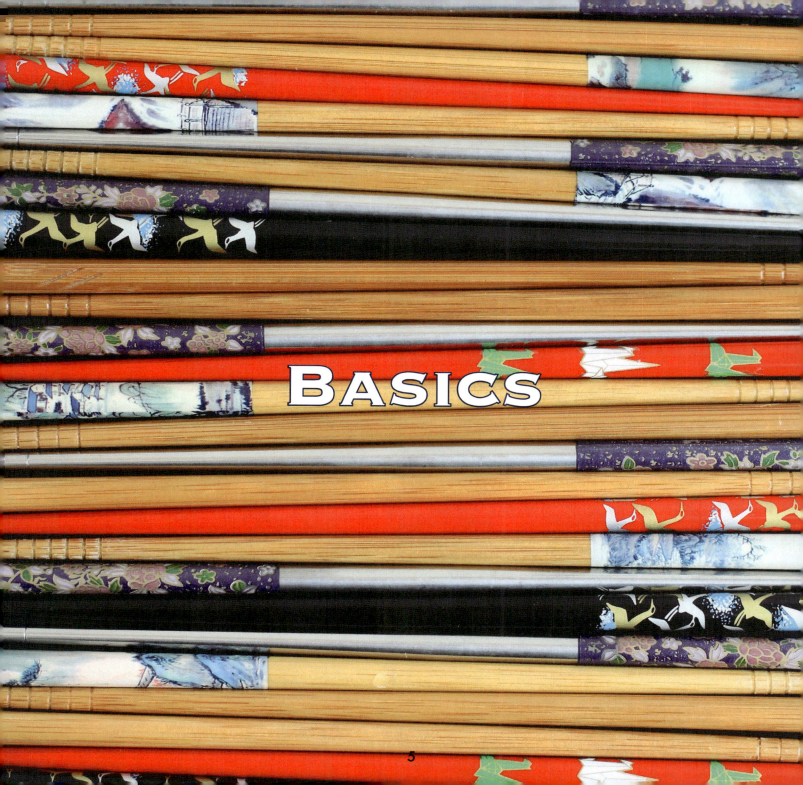
Basics

Every cuisine has its essentials, the basic components of a recipe that make their way into many of it's traditional meals. Latin cuisines all have their various versions of sofrito; the mix of garlic, onion, and tomato, and sometimes peppers or fresh herbs to make an aromatic base for sauces and salsas. The Thai make frequent use of fish sauce and small but fiery chilis, the French have their ever-present luxurious sauces, and who can forget the endless variations of spice blends in Indian cuisines? Japanese cooking is no different, with ubiquitous building blocks of its own. Mastering the use of these basics can boost confidence for cooking in a new style, wether it be with Japanese or with any cuisine.

Dashi

Dashi, also known as sea stock, is the base for most Japanese soups and stews. Rice is often boiled in dashi rather than water to add extra flavor and vitamins, and it's essential for making authentic miso soup. While you can buy a dried instant form of dashi, called hondashi, it is easy to make from scratch at home if you can find the right ingredients. Dried and shaved bonito flakes, called katsuobushi, along with kombu seaweed are all you need to make a basic stock. There are different permutations on the basic recipe, some using dried shiitake mushrooms, or even dried sardines or scallops, but the basic one is great for a variety of uses. Be careful never to let kombu boil though, as intense heat can make it slimy. A bare simmer is all that's needed to extract the salty and vegetal aromatics. Dashi has an earthy and unique flavor that is unlike any other stock in your pantry, but if you absolutely cannot find it or the ingredients to make it, you could substitute any stock you feel appropriate to compliment the recipe. It won't be the same without the distinctive flavor of dashi, but it will still be good.

6 cups water
a 4x4 inch piece of dried kombu
a heaping fistful of bonito flakes

Makes 6 cups

Or use 1 tsp. instant dried hondashi for every cup of water.

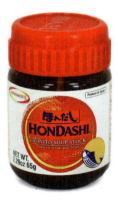

1. Place dried kombu in water in a medium sauce pot and let sit for 10 to 15 minutes to soften.
2. Turn heat onto medium high and allow to come up to a simmer. Wait one minute, then remove kombu with tongs.
3. Add katsuobushi and stir in. Allow to steep for 2 minutes.
4. Drain dashi into another container through a sieve lined with a tea cloth or paper towels to remove katsuobushi.
5. Use immediately or store in the refrigerator in a sealed container for up to 4 days.

STOVETOP SUSHI RICE

Rice is, without a doubt, the quintessential Japanese food. It is served with nearly every meal, and is often the meal itself. But the rice eaten in Japan is different from the rice most of us in the West are familiar with. I used to abhor the scoop of mushy white rice served with school lunches that would be absolutely flavorless save for the puddle of melted butter it sat in. And then there was the microwavable rice served at home, also fall-apart mushy and lacking any discernable flavor. Thankfully, the rice of Japan is not that rice. The Japanese eat a short grain variety with a higher gluten content than its long-grain cousin. It makes for a chewier texture, and the gluten encourages the grains to lightly stick to each other, allowing for easy eating with chopsticks. And as for flavor, there is a faint but present toasty aroma, and a starchiness that is reminiscent of fluffy steamed breads. Japanese short grain rice, sometimes sold as "sushi rice," is easy to make at home on the stovetop – no need for an expensive rice cooker, though if you have one you already know what an amazing and versatile tool it really is. Once you've mastered the art of making "good rice" you may find yourself craving it with every meal.

1 cup short grain white rice
1 cup water

Makes approx. 2 cups of cooked rice

1. Rinse rice in a mesh strainer under running water until water runs clear.
2. Place rice and water in a lidded pot that is at least twice the size of the contents.
3. Turn the heat on to high with the pot uncovered. As soon as the water starts to boil, put on the lid and turn the heat down to the lowest setting. Wait 15 minutes.
4. Take the pot off the heat entirely and wait another 10 minutes without removing the lid at any time.
5. Fluff rice with a rice paddle or spoon and serve. Keep covered to keep the rice from drying out.

SUSHI-SU

Short grain rice isn't technically sushi rice until it's been seasoned with sushi-su. "Su" means vinegar, so naturally, mellow rice vinegar is the base of this simple-to-prepare condiment. Sprinkle it over still warm cooked short grain rice, and gently fold in for a lightly tart and subtly sweet rice that perfectly compliments any fresh fish. I like to make a large batch of this recipe and keep it on hand in the refrigerator for ease of use, but it only takes a minute to whip up just enough for a serving of fresh homemade sushi.

1 tbsp. rice vinegar
1 tbsp. mirin
a three finger pinch of salt

Makes enough to season 2 cups of cooked sushi rice

1. Combine ingredients and stir to dissolve salt.
2. Store in a sealed container in the refrigerator for 6 months+.

花より団子

Hana yori dango

Food over flowers.

"It is more important to be well fed
than to be fancy."

- Japanese Proverb

Ingredients

Sushi Kome
Short Grain Rice

Rice comes in many shapes, flavors, and textures. The rice preferred in Japan is of the short grain variety, sometimes called glutinous rice or sushi rice. This type of rice is eaten nearly every day, either alone or as part of a larger dish. The grains stick together when cooked, allowing for easy eating with chopsticks. You can freeze extra cooked rice and reheat in the microwave easily, but the Japanese have developed many clever ways use up the leftover rice such as in the recipes to follow, which can be made either with fresh rice or with leftovers.

Before cooking, rinse rice under cool water until the water runs clear. This eliminates any excess starch that can make the final product gluey and soft.

Smoked Salmon Temari-zushi

I don't make a lot of sushi at home. It tends to be time-consuming, messy, and never as good as the stuff you get in a fancy restaurant prepared by a master chef. These temari-zushi are what I consider "casual sushi," dead simple to put together even with leftover ingredients and versatile enough to make for either a quick snack or an impressive appetizer for entertaining. Shaped to resemble the ornate fabric buttons on a geisha's kimono, these little hand-molded sushi may be simple to prepare but are incredibly beautiful, displayed like little jewels in a laquer box.

2 cups prepared sushi rice (pg.8)
1 tbsp. sushi-su (pg.9)
a 4oz. package of smoked salmon
1 lemon
black or blond sesame seeds for garnish

Makes approx. 12

1. In a wide bowl, sprinkle sushi-su over rice and lightly mix in using a rice paddle or spatula with cutting and folding motions.
2. Place a square of plastic wrap onto your prep surface and apply a small slice of smoked salmon onto the center of the plastic followed by a scoop of rice directly on top.
3. Pull the ends of the plastic up to meet each other and twist to enclose the salmon and rice in a balloon of plastic wrap.
4. Use your hands to wring the plastic wrap tighter and shape the sushi into a ball, then use your thumb to make a dimple in the top of the smoked salmon then unmold the sushi and set aside. Continue molding all the sushi before garnishing.
5. Cut lemon into wedges and use them to brush each temarizushi with juice. Sprinkle with sesame seeds if desired.
6. Temarizushi should be eaten at room temperature and should not be refrigerated as this will make the rice harden. Keep covered with a sheet of plastic wrap until ready to serve.

Chicken Okayu

When you get sick in the western world, you eat chicken noodle soup. When you get sick in Japan, you eat okayu. This rice porridge is eaten all over the Asian continent and goes by many names, but it's always mostly the same. Rice, usually left over from a previous meal, is boiled in water until soft then garnished with any number of flavorful toppings. In my interpretation, I've cooked the rice in chicken stock rather than water to make it richer and more comfortingly familiar. A hard-boiled chicken egg and sliced scallions top it off for flavor and texture.

2 cups cooked short grain rice (pg.8)
4 cups chicken stock
scallions and boiled egg to garnish (optional)

Makes approx. 6 cups

1. In a large lidded pot, bring stock to a boil and add cooked rice. Immediately turn heat down to medium low and cover.
2. Cook covered for 35 to 40 minutes, stirring every 10 minutes.
3. Serve hot with sliced scallions and boiled egg if desired.

Shoyu
Soy Sauce

Soy sauce is a dark, salty, liquid condiment used ubiquitously throughout Japanese cuisine. It is made by fermenting soybeans with water, salt, a live culture, and sometimes a grain such as wheat. It can be found in both dark (koikuchi) and light (usukuchi) varieties with the difference being that light soy sauce is both lighter in color and saltier. You'll find shoyu in soups, stews, dipping sauces, marinades, and glazes – anywhere salt is needed. Occasionally it even pops up in desserts, as a sticky glaze for rice dumplings when boiled with sugar.

There is a wheat-free version of soy sauce called tamari that can be enjoyed even by people with gluten intolerances.

Shoyu Tamago

There are so many ways to prepare an egg. Scrambled, omelet, sunny-side-up, over easy, baked, fried, poached, hard boiled, soft boiled – and if you're like me you'll eat them raw too. There is nothing more luxurious than a runny egg yolk dripping over toasted bread or adding richness to a hot broth. These soft-boiled shoyu tamago are easily adjustable to your preferred yolk firmness, whether you like them barely cooked or completely opaque. The salty glaze of soy sauce and sugar adds a deep salty flavor and aroma. They're wonderful as a snack on their own, or sliced in half in a bowl of hot noodle soup.

6 large eggs
1/4 cup dark soy sauce
1/8 cup mirin
2 tsp. sugar
ice and water

Makes 6

1. Bring water to a boil in a medium pot. Fill a separate bowl with ice water and set aside.
2. Slowly lower eggs into boiling water and allow to boil for exactly 6 minutes for a fully runny yolk, 8 minutes for half cooked, and up to 10 for fully opaque.
3. Remove eggs and plunge into the ice water bath. Allow to cool down completely before peeling.
4. Crack eggs one at a time by tapping them all over with gentle pressure on a hard, flat suface. Peel by working your finger under the membrane and lifting off the broken shell gently.
5. In a small saucepan, combine soy sauce, mirin, and sugar over medium heat.
6. Add eggs and swirl in the liquid for about 5 minutes making sure to keep them moving. Continually use a spoon to ladle the sauce over the eggs until they have reached a dark brown color.
7. Store in an air-tight container in the refrigerator for up to 4 days.

Honey-Soy Roast Beef Shoulder

Pot roast is one of the most comforting meals in Western cooking. A true "meat and potatoes" dish. Here, the classic gets updated with an Asian twist. Dark soy and sweet honey combine with the beef juices to form a rich and flavorful cooking liquid. Best of all, this roast is made in the slow cooker, so you can go about your day all the while knowing you're coming home to a comforting feast. The inevitable leftovers are also delightful as filling for Asian tacos, filled with a spicy cabbage slaw and sliced avocado.

a 2 and 1/2 pound boneless beef shoulder
1/4 cup soy sauce
1/4 cup honey

Serves 6 to 8

1. Trim beef shoulder of any large pieces of fat and cut into 2 or 3 pieces to fit in the slow cooker.
2. Pour over soy sauce and honey and cook on low for 8 hours, or on high for 6.
3. Pull apart meat slightly with tongs and separate from the cooking liquid.
4. Serve over mashed potatoes with a small amount of the reserved cooking liquid if desired. Store in an airtight container in the refrigerator for up to a week.

Miso
Fermented Soy Bean Paste

Miso is a thick paste made from fermented soybeans, sometimes mixed with rice or barley. It can range in color from nearly white to almost black depending on the combination of ingredients used. The flavor is mostly salty but some miso also display subtle sweetness and umami (savory) flavors as well. It is commonly used to flavor soups and stews and as a marinade or glaze for meats, but occasionally it can be found in desserts as well. It is usually sold in a sealable plastic container and can be kept in the refrigerator for many months without spoilage thanks to its active enzymes, though it should be used within 6 months to preserve its best flavor.

> When using miso in soups, press the paste through a mesh strainer with the back of a spoon to eliminate any clumps.

Miso-Glazed Salmon

Every household has their go-to recipes, the ones that are quick and easy to prepare and come out perfectly every time with minimal effort. This miso-glazed salmon is one of mine. The simple miso and mirin glaze comes together quickly in the microwave and the oven does the rest. It's truly a "set it and forget it" meal, but still manages to impress everyone who tries it. Sweet, tender salmon and salty miso are a perfect match. Serve with fluffy rice, steamed bok choy, and if you really want something special – slices of ripe avocado.

a 15 oz. piece of salmon (steak or fillet)
1 heaped tbsp. red or white miso paste
1 tbsp. mirin
sesame seeds to garnish

Serves 2

1. Line a baking sheet with aluminum foil and preheat oven to 400°F.
2. Blot salmon dry with a paper towel and lay on the baking sheet. Check for any pinbones and remove.
3. In a small dish, microwave miso and mirin together for around 15 to 20 seconds, just long enough to warm it. Stir to make a paste.
4. Spread miso mixture evenly over the piece of salmon.
5. Bake for 20 to 22 minutes. Do not worry if you notice any burnt black crust on the foil, the salmon will not be affected by it and the foil will protect the baking sheet.
6. Garnish with sesame seeds if desired.

Miso Soup

It's a classic, a dish you'll find in any Japanese restaurant. The comfort and warmth of this simple soup can be recreated at home authentically with just a few ingredients, but if you can't get your hands on dashi stock or the ingredients to make it, you can substitute vegetable stock for a similar and equally satisfying broth. Feel free to play around with the add-ins too. Button mushooms and shredded chicken can easily stand in for shiitakes and tofu in a pinch. What's important here is the rich and salty miso paste dissolved into the hot broth. There's something mesmerizing about the way it settles to the bottom of the bowl and then swirls up in a cloud with the swish of your spoon. This is what I crave on a cold day, a hot and flavorful soup to put the color back in my cheeks. It's a warm blanket in a bowl.

4 cups dashi stock (pg.7)
3 tbsp. white miso paste
1/2 a block of silken tofu cut into small cubes
4 to 6 small shiitake mushroom caps (sliced thinly)
3 scallions (sliced thinly)

Serves 4 to 6

1. Heat dashi stock over medium heat. Do not allow to come to a boil as this can give dashi a filmy quality.
2. Whisk in miso paste then add all other ingredients. Take care to stir softly so as not to break apart the delicate silken tofu.
3. Allow to come back up to a bare simmer before serving.

Mirin
Sweet Rice Seasoning

Mirin is a sweet liquid condiment that is made in much the same way as sake but contains a very low alcohol content. It is nearly half sugar, so it is used as a sweetener in many dishes. It is more than just a simple sugar syrup though. Mirin contains the active culture koji, which gives it a distinct dry flavor one might associate with white wine, but with a golden, almost buttery subtle sweetness. Mirin is one of the main ingredients in both ponzu and teriyaki sauces. It pairs well with oily fishes where it helps to mask any strong smells, and can be used in place of sugar in any sauce.

Most of the mirin you find in grocery stores is an imitation. Be sure to read the ingredient label to find one made with real koji culture for the most authentic flavor.

Mirin-Glazed Roasted Carrots

I love the natural sweetness that comes out of vegetables when roasted. I love the smoky little burned edges and the soft texture that even the toughest roots seem to relax into. Carrots especially are improved by this method, and are even better when their earthy sweetness is paired with a complimentary glaze. Here, I've bathed them in sweet mirin, for a dry almost white-wine like aroma and light sugary caramelization. They are excellent alongside a Honey-Soy Roast Beef Shoulder - found on pg.17 of this book, or with your favorite main course.

8 to 10 medium-sized carrots
1 to 2 tbsp. canola oil
1/4 cup mirin
1 tbsp. sesame seeds

Serves 3 to 4

1. Rinse carrots and scrub off fibers with a stiff-bristled brush. Do not peel.
2. Cut off carrot tops and slice in half lengthwise.
3. Arrange on a baking sheet and rub all over with canola oil.
4. Use a pastry brush to brush on half of the mirin.
5. Roast in a 400°F oven for 30 minutes, brushing on the remaining mirin 10 minutes before the end of roasting. Sprinkle with sesame seeds while carrots are still hot.

Sweet Cotton Omelet

I'd bet that when you think of eggs, the words "sweet" or "dessert" are not ones that come to mind. But if you've ever had the tamago omelet that comes at the end of a sushi dinner, you know that eggs can indeed be sweet, even deliciously so. This breakfast omelet seeks to recreate the sweet flavor of sushi tamago with the addition of mirin, which is precisely what gives tamago its syrupy sweetness. Beaten egg whites give it a pillowy texture akin to fresh-baked breakfast pastries. Top with the contrasting bite of chopped scallions, or the lightest dusting of powdered sugar to bring out its sweet flavor.

4 large eggs
1/4 cup mirin
1/2 tsp. baking soda
pinch of salt
a flavorless non-stick spray

Serves 4 to 6

1. Separate eggs with the whites in a large mixing bowl and the yolks in a smaller bowl. Whisk yolks until smooth.
2. Whisk egg whites with the mirin, salt, and baking soda by hand or with a mixer until soft peaks form.
3. Gently fold the yolks into the whites with a rubber spatula.
4. Spray an oven-safe skillet with non-stick spray and heat over medium-high heat.
5. Gently add egg mixture to the pan and smooth out the top.
6. Cook for 4 minutes, then transfer entire skillet to a preheated 350°F oven to cook for an additional 10 minutes.
7. Allow omelet to cool in skillet for 5 minutes, then slide out or invert onto a serving plate and slice to serve.

Komezu
Rice Vinegar

Komezu is a combination of the Japanese words for rice (kome) and vinegar (su.) This is a very sweet and mildly acidic vinegar made from rice that can be used for salad dressings, as a masking agent for strong-smelling fishes such as mackerel, and especially for making pickles. Pickled vegetables of all kinds, commonly referred to as tsukemono, are a very popular Japanese condiment served alongside many dishes. Rice vinegar is perfect for making these pickles because its mild flavor allows the flavor of the vegetable to shine through. Because this vinegar is so mild, it is not appropriate to substitute another type of vinegar, such as white or apple cider varieties, as these are too harshly acidic to recreate the same subtle flavor.

> Rice vinegar is excellent for pickling fruits, as its milder flavor doesn't overpower the fruits natural sweetness.

Mango Salad with Grapefruit Ginger Vinaigrette

Making your own salad dressings at home is extremely simple, especially if you employ the mason jar method – add all ingredients to the jar, seal, and shake like mad. This time, I've combined two flavors that I'm absolutely obsessed with right now, grapefruit and ginger. Tart and slightly spicy, with just the right amount of mellow acidity from the rice vinegar, this dressing cuts through the fattiness of the creamy avocados and contrasts with the sweet sliced mango in this refreshing salad. With a sprinkling of bitter cilantro on top, it's a salad that hits every part of the palate. Sour. Sweet. Bitter. Salty. Fatty. Spicy.

4 large romaine leaves
half a mango
half an avocado
a small handful of fresh cilantro
1/2 cup fresh-squeezed grapefruit juice
1 tbsp. rice vinegar
3 tbsp. canola or sesame oil
salt and cracked black pepper to taste

Serves 1 to 2

1. Slice romaine leaves lengthwise through the ribs and chop into small pieces. Arrange slices of mango and avocado around the outside of the plate and top with cilantro.
2. In a mason jar or other sealed container, combine juice, rice vinegar, salt and pepper. Shake to combine.
3. Pour desired amount over salad. Store remaining dressing in a sealed container in the refrigerator for up to a week.

Spicy Cucumber Quick Pickles

Nothing beats the traditional cucumber pickle. Sour and crunchy, it serves as a palate cleanser between bites of our favorite summertime cookout foods. These tangy little cukes are puckered up with rice vinegar and have a tingly spiciness that might just make you sweat. I love to serve them as a refreshing condiment alongside grilled meats or tossed over an otherwise lackluster salad. It's a punchy little pickle that's quick to fix.

3 small cucumbers
1 medium carrot (grated)
1 scallion (chopped)
2 tsp. sesame seeds
1 tbsp. rice vinegar
1 tsp. mirin
1/2 tsp. chili garlic sauce
salt

Makes approx. 1 cup
to a cup and a half

1. Slice cucumbers thinly and place in a bowl. Sprinkle with salt and allow to sit for 15 minutes.
2. Drain liquid from cucumbers and lightly squeeze out more of the moisture. Transfer to a clean bowl.
3. Add grated carrot and chopped scallion to cucumbers. Pour over vinegar, mirin, and chili garlic sauce and toss to combine. Garnish with sesame seeds.
4. Store in an air-tight container in the refrigerator for up to 2 weeks.

Sake
Fermented Rice Alcohol

Sake is often referred to in the West as rice wine, however, this fermented beverage is not actually a wine at all, it's brewing process being more similar to that of beer. Rice is boiled and some of it is inoculated with a type of mold called koji, which converts the starches into sugars. It is then mixed with water and yeast to form the mash and is left to ferment. After filtering out the solids known as kasu, the strong alcohol is diluted to the correct percentage and bottled. It is often served in a small wooden box, called a masu, or in a small cup poured to overflowing. Sake can be used for cooking in any way you would typically use white wine and pairs best with chicken, fish, and shellfish.

> A bottle of sake will start to oxidize after opening and begin changing flavor after about 2 to 3 days. A great way to use up leftover sake that has oxidized is to serve it hot.

Sake-Steamed Mussels

The hardest part about making mussels is getting them home alive. Once they're safe at home and freshly scrubbed, it's mere minutes before they're ready to eat. The only part that isn't foolproof is figuring out what to flavor them with. White wine is a common steaming liquid for mussels, so sake seemed like an apt replacement to create a distinctly Asian flavor. I steamed these little blue-lipped beauties with a dry sake and asian-flavored broth and they turned out lovely. The best part is soaking up the leftover broth, now infused with the oceanic shellfish liquor, with a crusty piece of grilled bread.

2 lbs. mussels
1 large leek
3 large garlic cloves (thinly sliced)
2 tbsp. butter
1 tbsp. canola oil

1 cup sake
1 cup dashi (pg.7)
1 tbsp. mirin
2 tsp. soy sauce

Serves 2 to 4

1. Purchase your mussels the day you want to use them and keep them on ice until ready to use.
2. Scrub each mussel under running water with a stiff bristled brush and pull out or trim the beards. Some mussels may be slightly open but should be fine as long as they don't smell bad or have broken shells.
3. Slice leek in half and then into half rounds, stopping a quarter way into the darkest green parts. Rinse leeks in a strainer under cool running water to wash out any sand or dirt.
4. In a large lidded pot over medium heat, saute leeks and garlic in butter and oil until soft.
5. Add mussels and sake and stir. Immediately turn the heat to medium high. Add dashi, mirin, and soy sauce, and put on the lid.
6. Let mussels steam for 5 minutes with the lid on. If all the mussels appear to be open after 5 minutes, go ahead and serve them. If a few are still just barely open, give them up to 2 more minutes with the lid on. Any mussels not open after that time should be discarded.
7. Serve with toasted bread to sop up the sake-scented cooking liquid.

Sake Risotto with Seared Scallops

Risotto isn't all that difficult to make at home, and yet every time I begin to crave it I end up convincing myself that it's too much of an enterprise. Who has time for all that stirring? And yet every time I do endeavor to make it I'm reminded that it really isn't too much work. I really have no excuse with this sake risotto, which uses short grain sushi rice in lieu of the traditional arborio rice. Not only does the short grain rice cook up quicker, but it also provides plenty of creaminess from its hefty gluten content, and without as much frantic stirring. The dry sake flavor really comes through here, and is a perfect compliment to sweet seared scallops, or your favorite fresh fish.

Serves 2

3/4 cup uncooked short grain sushi rice
2 and 1/2 cups dashi (pg.7)
4 scallions (sliced thinly)
6 large shiitake mushroom caps (chopped)
3/4 cup sake

6 large scallops
sprinkle of salt
a flavorless oil such as canola
squeeze of lemon (optional)

1. Rinse scallops and pat dry. Season all over with salt and set aside.
2. Heat 3 tbsp. of oil in a large pot and add thinly sliced scallions and shiitakes. Stir for one minute or until soft.
3. Rinse rice in a mesh strainer until water runs clear then drain and add to pot. Allow to toast in the oil for about 2 minutes.
4. Turn off the heat, add sake, then turn the heat back on to just above medium.
5. Start by adding a half cup or so of dashi and stir continuously until the rice has absorbed most of the liquid. Continue adding liquid in this fashion until all the liquid is used.
6. In a non-stick pan, heat 2 tbsp. oil over medium heat. Add scallops and cook for 3-4 minutes on each side or until scallops are seared golden brown on both sides and springy but firm to the touch. Serve over risotto with a squeeze of lemon juice if desired.

Wasabi
Japanese Horseradish

You may be familiar with that little green dab on the corner of sushi plates known as wasabi, but did you know that the wasabi we're familiar with in the States is usually just regular horseradish and food coloring? The real wasabi, a rhizome that grows in wet areas of Japan, is difficult to cultivate and therefore fetches a high price tag. For this reason, it's rarely exported. While the real stuff is made by grating the root on a sharkskin grater called an oroshigane, the horseradish-based pastes and powders you can find in most supermarkets will work just fine. Wasabi does not stand up well to high heat, and its flavor will also diminish when left exposed to air for longer than 20 minutes.

> Be careful not to let wasabi touch anything that you don't want to taste like wasabi. A little goes a long way and even a speck can turn something sweet into a spicy surprise.

Wasabi Party Cheese Ball

Any time there's a party, you can be sure to find me parked in front of the refreshment table monopolizing the cheese plate. I'm notorious for making a meal out of little bits of cured meats, pungent cheeses, and succulent jams, all slathered on the closest carbohydrate. This spicy little wasabi cheese ball is one I'd gladly plant myself in front of and make a major dent in. The wasabi flavor is bright and vegetal. It has just the right amount of heat balanced with the cooling cream cheese and is perfect with a little curl of smoked salmon on top of a crisp cracker. It's sure to spice up any party platter, and don't forget to spread the leftovers on your morning bagel.

2 8oz. packages of cream cheese (softened)
3 tbsp. wasabi puree
3 scallions (sliced thinly)
2 drops green food coloring (optional)
6 tbsp. sesame seeds (any color)

Serves a crowd of 10+

1. Beat softened cream cheese, wasabi puree, scallions, and food coloring in a mixer until fully incorporated.
2. Scoop mixture onto a sheet of plastic wrap and twist into a ball.
3. Refrigerate for at least 4 hours or freeze for 1 hour.
4. Pour sesame seeds into a large bowl and roll the cheese ball in them until completely covered. Use your hands to work the ball into a perfectly round shape.
5. Serve with crackers and smoked salmon if desired.

Creamy Wasabi Potato Salad

Love it or hate it, potato salad is a summertime staple. You'll find it at every picnic and barbecue, and every mother or grandmother or aunt has their own idea about how to make a good one. For me, a good one means big chunks of yukon gold potatoes, no eggs, and very little mayo - call me crazy, but I like to actually taste the potatoes. My version of the classic potato salad is lightly dressed with a sour cream-based dressing, and gets spruced up with the spicy crunch of fresh scallions and just enough heat from the wasabi to turn on the perspiration. If it's true that spicy food cools you down in hot weather, then this dish should chill you out in no time.

2 lbs. yukon gold potatoes
1/3 cup sour cream
2 tbsp. mayo
1 and 1/2 tsp. wasabi puree
1/2 tsp. salt
4 to 6 thinly sliced scallions
1 tbsp. sesame seeds

Serves 8 to 10

1. Chop potatoes to desired size and boil in water until tender enough that when pierced with a fork they almost split apart.
2. Drain potatoes and run under cool water to stop the cooking process. Transfer to a large mixing bowl and allow to cool completely before adding other ingredients.
3. In a small bowl, mix together all other ingredients then add to the cooled potatoes and stir in gently.
4. Serve at room temperature or cooled in the refrigerator as preferred.

Tofu
Soy Bean Curd

Like many Japanese food products, tofu came to Japan by way of China. Tofu is made by coagulating soymilk with salts and acids to create curds, much like in cheese-making. For silken tofu, the soymilk is coagulated directly in the container it is to be sold in and none of the liquid is removed, whereas with firm tofu, the curds are cut and pressed into blocks, removing some of the liquid for a firmer product. Tofu is not seen as a meat replacement by the Japanese but as a truly unique and versatile food on its own. You'll find it in soups, baked or fried, marinated, or even used as a creamy dessert base for puddings or pies.

> Before cooking tofu, it is important to squeeze out the excess liquid so that it can become crispy. You can use a tofu press, or simply wrap the tofu in a tea cloth and press under a heavy object.

HIYAYAKKO

It's always nice to eat something cool and refreshing in the summertime. Salads of crisp lettuces, fresh fruit, or pasta with crisp veggies and creamy sauce are all stand-bys. Here's one more salad to add to your repertoire. Hiyayakko is nothing more than cold silken tofu in soy sauce and topped with whatever's fresh and flavorful at the time. Traditional toppings include scallions, grated ginger, and dried bonito flake, and that's exactly what I've chosen for my version of this recipe. However, the options for dressing this luscious cold tofu are endless. Try supremes of citrus fruits in a sweet syrup; basil chiffonade, roasted tomatoes, and balsamic vinegar; or marinated mushrooms in a tangy vinaigrette. Cool and creamy silken tofu is the perfect blank canvas for any summer salad you can imagine.

1 block silken tofu
1 tbsp. + 1 tsp. soy sauce
3 scallions (sliced thinly)
a 1 inch piece of ginger (grated)
sprinkle of dried bonito flake (optional)

Serves 2 to 4

1. Open tofu container and drain out any excess liquid.
2. Scoop spoonfuls of tofu onto a plate and drizzle with soy sauce.
3. Garnish with sliced scallions, grated ginger, and dried bonito flake if desired.
4. Serve chilled.

TAHINI-MISO BAKED TOFU

While tofu is seen by the Japanese as much more than a meat replacement, it still works well as the centerpiece of a meal. Baked firm tofu is a great "blank canvas" meal starter that can be transformed by whatever sauce or marinade it's basted with. The tahini-miso sauce in this tofu dish bakes up to a golden crackled shell with the flavors of toasted sesame and umami miso. The rich flavor coats the firm and chewy baked tofu with its crispy edges and soft center. Served with rice and steamed baby bok choy, it's a meatless meal that's sure to please.

2 blocks firm tofu
1/4 cup tahini
1 tbsp. miso paste
2 tbsp. mirin
2 tbsp. water
1 tbsp. lemon juice

Serves 4

1. Slice blocks of tofu lengthwise into 6 slices each.
2. Lay slices between layers of a clean kitchen towel or teacloth and weigh down with something heavy to squeeze excess moisture out. Let sit for 10 minutes.
3. In a small bowl, combine tahini, miso, water, and lemon juice and whisk with a fork.
4. Line a baking sheet with foil and spray lightly with non-stick cooking spray. Arrange tofu slices on baking sheet and coat each with a thin layer of the tahini-miso mixture.
5. Bake at 400°F for 25 minutes. Serve with rice and sauteed bok choy if desired.

Goma
Sesame Seeds

When you think of sesame seeds you probably think of the white variety, but sesame seeds can range in color anywhere from a pale cream to the darkest black. They have a lightly nutty flavor which is amplified by toasting. Sesame seeds are also prized for the rich oil they produce, which stands up well to heat and is resistant to rancidity for longer than many other common cooking oils. The seeds grow in pods on a flowering plant that thrives mostly in Africa and India. In fact, though Japan is the world's largest importer of sesame products, very little is grown there as it fares better in drier climates. The seeds are a common garnish for many Japanese dishes and are sometimes even ground into a paste, known elsewhere in the world as tahini, for use in sauces and broths.

> Sesame seeds are prone to rancidity. For the longest lasting seeds, store in the refrigerator or freezer and only keep enough out to fill a spice shaker.

Sesame Kara-Age

Kara-age, also known as tatsuta-age, is Japanese style fried chicken. Juicy chicken thighs are marinated in soy and ginger and traditionally get coated with potato starch before frying. I've substituted corn starch here and added a heaping helping of sesame seeds that toast up to a golden nuttiness in the fryer. Serve these as the Japanese do, with a squeeze of lemon and mayo for dipping, or pair them with your favorite sauce for a pop-able snack.

4 boneless and skinless chicken thighs (about 1 lb.)
2 tbsp. soy sauce
1 tbsp. mirin
1 tsp. freshly-grated ginger
1/2 cup corn starch
1/2 cup sesame seeds
approx. 2 cups vegetable oil

Serves 4

1. Trim chicken of excess fat and chop into approx. 1 inch pieces.
2. Allow chicken pieces to marinate in soy sauce, mirin, and ginger for 30 minutes at room temperature.
3. In a bowl, combine corn starch and sesame seeds. Toss chicken pieces in the corn starch mixture to coat.
4. Heat oil in a deep pan to just above medium heat. Add coated chicken in small batches and allow to fry for 2 minutes.
5. Transfer chicken to a cooling rack lined with paper towels to absorb excess oil.

TOASTED SESAME BLONDIES

At first bite, the flavor of these golden chewy blondies is reminiscent of roasted peanut butter, but soon fills your mouth and nose with the distinctive nutty aroma of toasted sesame. These little sweets manage to be both crumbly and soft at the same time, a perfect dessert or snack served warm with vanilla ice cream or alone.

Makes approx. 18

1 and 1/2 sticks melted butter
1 and 3/4 cups packed brown sugar
2 large eggs
1/2 tsp. vanilla extract
2 cups all-purpose flour

2 tsp. baking powder
pinch of salt
1 cup sesame seeds
+1 tbsp. sesame seeds for garnish

1. Toast 1 cup of sesame seeds in a dry pan over medium heat for about ten minutes or until fragrant and lightly browned.
2. Pulse toasted sesame seeds and brown sugar together in a food processor, then drizzle in melted butter and pulse again to combine.
3. Transfer sesame butter to a large mixing bowl and add in vanilla and eggs, stir to combine.
4. In a separate bowl, whisk together flour, baking powder, and salt. Add to wet mixture in three additions, mixing completely between each.
5. Add batter to an ungreased 9x13 inch baking dish. It will be very thick and you may need to use your hands to push it into the corners and even out the surface.
6. Sprinkle over the extra tablespoon of sesame seeds and pat in lightly.
7. Bake in a preheated 350°F oven for 25 to 30 minutes, or until a knife inserted in the center comes out clean. Let cool completely in baking dish.
8. Cut into squares while still in the baking dish and serve. Store in an airtight container.

PANKO
JAPANESE BREAD CRUMBS

Panko breadcrumbs are nothing like their Italian or homemade counterparts. They are almost always made with a crustless white bread baked specifically for making panko and are much more coarsely ground, even flaky. They are a favorite for coating fried foods because they absorb less oil than traditional breadcrumbs and stay crunchy longer. Panko also has no real flavor of its own, allowing the flavors of the food it coats to shine through, but seasonings will stick to it well if you desire to flavor it. Try replacing regular breadcrumbs with panko any time you need that extra crunch.

> Store panko in an air-tight container to avoid staleness and to retain its crisp crunchiness.

Korokke

Korokke is a Japanese approximation of the word "croquette," a little fried snack of mashed potatoes with any number of fillings and seasonings. These scrumptious croquettes are filled with a mixture of mashed potato and ground beef. They are delightfully crunchy on the outside and soft and comforting on the inside. A few of them can make for a meal on their own, drizzled with tonkatsu sauce or spicy mustard, or as a quick snack after being re-crisped in the toaster oven.

1 lb. yukon gold potatoes
1/2 lb. lean ground beef
half a large onion (diced)
1 egg
1 tsp. salt

6 to 8 cracks freshly ground black pepper (1/4 tsp.)
2 cups panko bread crumbs
1/2 cup flour to dredge
2 eggs for coating
canola oil for frying

Makes 8 to 10

1. Peel and chop potatoes then boil until tender and drain. Return to the pot and toss with a spoon over medium heat for 2 to 3 minutes to evaporate some of the excess moisture.
2. Mash potatoes in a large bowl with salt and pepper.
3. Saute diced onion in canola oil over medium heat until soft.
4. Add in ground beef and chop into small pieces with a spoon until broken into small crumbles. Continue cooking beef until most of the moisture has cooked off.
5. Add beef and onions to mashed potatoes and incorporate with a potato masher. Allow mixture to cool for 5 minutes before adding one egg and mixing through.
6. With your hands, form the mixture into small patties then dredge in flour and set aside.
7. In a small bowl, whisk remaining two eggs and use to dip patties in before coating in panko.
8. Heat enough canola oil to cover the bottom of a non-stick pan over medium-high heat.
9. Fry croquettes on both sides a few at a time until golden brown. Allow to cool on a cooling rack.
10. Serve with tonkatsu sauce or your favorite dipping sauce.
11. Store in an airtight container in the refrigerator and reheat in a toaster oven for 5 minutes.

TONKATSU

This crunchy breaded pork cutlet is a staple of Japanese cooking. You can find it on top of rice, served atop a rich curry, or even garnishing a bowl of noodles. When served alone, it is always accompanied by its own special tonkatsu dipping sauce, a blend of ketchup, worcestershire, and soy sauce. The pork remains pink and juicy and the panko crisps up to a golden crunch. Never too greasy and always delicious.

Serves 2

2 boneless pork chops
1 cup or so panko breadcrumbs
2 eggs
2 tbsp. milk (or water)

salt and pepper to season
3 tbsp. sesame oil for frying
tonkatsu sauce (or hoisin) for dipping

1. Trim pork chops of any extra fat and pound with a meat mallet between layers of plastic wrap until they are approximately a half inch thick. Salt and pepper lightly on both sides.
2. In a shallow bowl, whisk eggs and milk together. Pour panko onto a large plate and crush it a bit with the bottom of a drinking glass so that some of it is a fine powder and some is still large crumbs.
3. Dip pork chops in egg mixture and coat completely. Transfer to plate of panko crumbs and cover completely. It helps to pick up a handful of crumbs and crush them over the top of the pork chop and pat in. Keep rotating and adding more crumbs until it looks well covered.
4. Heat sesame oil in a pan to just over medium heat.
5. Fry pork chops in the oil for approximately 4 to 5 minutes on each side, or until a golden brown color is achieved.
6. Let cool on a cooling rack or paper towels to absorb excess oil before slicing.
7. Serve with tonkatsu sauce, or if you can't find it, hoisin or your favorite steak sauce.

Ramen
Fried Instant Noodles

Ramen, or instant noodles, are thin wheat noodles that have been flash fried. They are most often sold in cheap individual-sized packages and cook quickly in just a few minutes. While ramen noodles are relatively common in the West, especially with students on tight budgets, the way they are enjoyed in Japan is a much different experience. Every region of Japan has a favorite ramen recipe; some served with thick slabs of roasted pork belly or sliced raw beef, some with thin clear broths and others in rich stocks made from miso and fatty bone marrow, and always with an assortment of stewed vegetables and flavorful condiments.

> Toss out the seasoning packet that comes with ramen, high in sodium and other unpleasantries, and instead cook the noodles in a stock and add vegetables and flavorings to your liking.

SESAME BROTH RAMEN WITH BACON

My favorite ramen is undoubtedly the tonkotsu style, which features a milky broth flavored by pork bones that have boiled for hours and hours to extract their rich marrow and collagen. It's often served with a big hunk of fatty pork belly, a barely cooked egg, and in recent years has frequently been infused with the flavor of toasted sesame seeds. Making a real tonkotsu ramen is a labor of love with hours spent perfecting the rich pork stock it's famous for. I affectionately call this version my "cheater's tonkotsu" with its creamy sesame tahini broth and bacon in place of pork belly. It's great with a shoyu tamago (pg.16) sliced in half, oozing its half-cooked yolk over the noodles. A true ramen lover may cry sacrilege to call this a tonkotsu, but if you squint really hard you might just see a glimpse of the real thing in this quick-and-dirty home version.

2 individual packages instant ramen noodles (minus the seasoning packets)
2 cups vegetable stock or broth
1 cup dashi (pg.7)
3 tbsp. tahini
2 tsp. miso paste
1/2 tsp. soy sauce
1/4 tsp. chili garlic sauce
2 slices unsmoked lean bacon
2 scallions (sliced)
sesame seeds for garnish

Serves 2

1. Heat vegetable stock, dashi, and soy sauce over medium high heat. Lightly whisk in tahini, miso, and chili garlic sauce.
2. Add in bacon slices and instant ramen noodles and boil according to package directions (usually about 3 minutes.)
3. Garnish with sliced scallions and sesame seeds.

Black Pepper Chicken Ramen

Here's an unusual ramen recipe. Rather than the rich stocks and fatty cuts of meat found in typical authentic ramen, this one is light and refreshing with a clear chicken stock, squeeze of lemon, and a few hefty cracks of sinus-opening black pepper. Juicy roast chicken still encased in its crispy skin is the centerpiece. It's chicken noodle soup in a way you've never seen it before, but just as comforting.

2 small bone-in skin-on chicken breasts
3 cups chicken stock
1 tsp. soy sauce
juice of a lemon wedge (an 8th of a lemon)
8 to 10 generous cracks of freshly ground black pepper (1/4 tsp.)
2 individual packages ramen noodles (minus the seasoning packets)
salt, pepper, and olive oil for roasting chicken

scallions and chili garlic sauce to garnish

Serves 2

1. Dry chicken breasts thoroughly with a paper towel. Sprinkle all over with salt and pepper and rub with olive oil.
2. Bake chicken skin-side-up on a baking sheet lined with parchment paper or foil for 40 minutes at 400°F.
3. When chicken is roasted and has cooled, slice the breasts off the bone in one large piece and slice into strips.
4. In a medium pot combine stock, soy sauce, lemon juice, and cracked black pepper and allow to come up to a boil. Add ramen noodles and cook according to package directions (usually 3 minutes.)
5. Serve topped with the sliced chicken and garnish with scallions and a small pinch of chili garlic sauce if desired.

Soba
Buckwheat Noodles

Soba are thin dark noodles made from buckwheat flour. These are usually served cold on a bamboo tray called a zaru, and accompanied by an intensely flavored dipping sauce and other toppings. Sometimes these can be found in hot soups in the winter months, but the cold preparation is favored, as it allows the eater to taste the nutty and slightly sweet flavor of the buckwheat noodles alone and enjoy their chewy texture. Soba is usually sold dried and cooks up like spaghetti in boiling water. Use it in place of whole wheat noodles in any pasta dish.

After boiling, rinse cooked soba under cool water to stop the cooking process to retain its chewiness.

Caramelized Onion Soba

It's rare to find soba served hot. Rich broths and sauces just cover up the subtle flavor of the buckwheat rather than compliment it. In this hot soba dish, I've paired the nutty soba with sweet caramelized onion. The flavors enhance each other, rather than fighting for the starring role, and both soak up just enough of the honey-soy sauce. I love this with a little piece of seared salmon on top, but it's fantastic on its own or as a side dish.

2 portions dried soba noodles
1 large yellow onion
4 tbsp. soy sauce
1 tbsp. honey
2-3 tbsp. canola oil

Serves 2 to 4

1. Cut onion in half and slice into half rings. Saute in oil over medium heat until soft and browned.
2. Meanwhile, boil soba according to package directions (usually about 4 minutes) and drain. Reserve about half a cup or so of the pasta water.
3. Add soba, soy sauce, and honey to the onions and toss together over low heat. Add some of the reserved pasta water a few tablespoons at a time to thin out the sauce if needed.
4. Serve immediately while still hot.

Chilled Zaru-soba with Mentsuyu Dipping Sauce

This is the classic, the original, the best way to enjoy soba as it's meant to be eaten. The noodles are cooked to al dente and plunged into ice water to halt the cooking process. They're served solo, ice cold, with optional toppings and a side of hot soup for dipping. The noodles have a springy chewiness that is a true delight to eat, and the mentsuyu soup is little more than dashi stock flavored with soy sauce -- it never overpowers the subtle buckwheat flavor of the soba. There's also something fun about dipping each bite of noodles into the mentsuyu and then slurping them up making as much noise as you can. It's great as a light summertime lunch to cool you down while you're filling up.

approx. 6 oz. soba noodles
1 and 1/2 cups dashi (pg.7)
2 tbsp. soy sauce
1 tbsp. mirin
2 scallions (sliced thinly)
shredded nori for garnish

Serves 2

1. In a small sauce pot over medium heat, add water, hondashi, soy sauce, and mirin. Whisk to dissolve.
2. Boil soba according to package directions (usually about 4 minutes), drain, and immediately add to a bath of ice water.
3. Drain soba and serve while still cold. Garnish with shredded nori and sliced scallions if desired.
4. To eat, dip noodles one mouthful at a time into mentsuyu dipping sauce and slurp up.

Udon
Thick Wheat Noodles

Udon are thick wheat noodles used in hot soups or served chilled, much like soba. They are soft, slightly chewy, and mostly flavorless, so they work well in rich broths. Udon are sometimes sold dried and sometimes pre-cooked and sealed in plastic, but it is not uncommon for people to still make them fresh at home. The dough is made with nothing more than flour, water and salt, but the process is where it gets really interesting. The dough ball is placed in a plastic bag and gets kneaded with your feet! The low liquid content of the dough makes it much too difficult to knead by hand. Watch out for portions before you boil them, as udon noodles usually double in size during cooking.

> Overcooking udon will cause the noodles to break apart. As with most noodles, al dente is best.

Tsukimi Udon

Tsukimi means "moon viewing" and refers to the several Japanese festivals centered around viewing the autumn moon. In this dish a raw egg is cracked over a hot udon soup, the yolk symbolizing the full harvest moon. You can choose to mix the egg in to the soup, creating a creamy broth, or allow the yolk to coat the noodles in velvety richness as you drag them through it. Though the dish was created to be eaten at the moon viewing festivals, it is enjoyed year round.

2 cups dashi (pg.7)
1 cup vegetable stock
2 tsp. mirin
2 tsp. soy sauce
2 tbsp. miso paste
2 individual packages of udon noodles
2 eggs at room temperature
2 sliced scallions for garnish

Serves 2

1. Combine dashi, vegetable stock, mirin, and soy sauce in a pot and heat to boiling. Whisk in miso paste until dissolved.
2. Add udon noodles and cook to package directions (usually 3 minutes.)
3. Quickly transfer noodles and broth into serving bowls and crack an egg over each portion. Immediately cover bowls with an upside-down plate and wait 5 minutes for the eggs to partially cook.
4. Top with sliced scallions and use chopsticks to whisk any remaining uncooked egg into the broth to make it creamy, or enjoy as is.

Yaki-Udon

Any time you find the word "yaki" in a Japanese dish you can expect something that has been either grilled over charcoal or cooked on a super-hot griddle. We all know how good grilled food is, but have you ever heard of grilling noodles? In this "yaki," chewy udon noodles are cooked in a hot cast iron skillet along with seared slices of beef and caramelized onions and peppers, all in a sweet and salty sauce. It's a stir-fry. It's noodles. It's both.

Serves 4

1/2 lb. flank steak
1 small onion
1 small red bell pepper
14 oz. udon noodles
2 tbsp. soy sauce
1 tbsp. mirin
1 tsp. sugar
1 tbsp. canola oil
sliced scallion for garnish

1. Slice flank steak as thinly as possible across the grain and set aside.
2. Pour oil into a cast iron skillet and use a paper towel to brush it across the bottom and up the sides. Bring skillet up to medium heat. Meanwhile, bring a pot of water up to a boil.
3. Slice onion into half rings and bell pepper into thin strips. Saute in the hot oil until onions begin to caramelize.
4. Push vegetables to the side of the skillet and sear the flank steak on both sides.
5. Boil udon according to package directions (usually 3 minutes). Drain and add to the skillet.
6. Add soy sauce, mirin, and sugar and toss together until the noodles have absorbed most of the liquid.
7. Serve hot with sliced scallions for garnish if desired.

Nori
Seaweed Paper

Nori is the Japanese word for seaweed and therefore can refer to any edible seaweed. Usually though, when people speak of nori, they mean the thin, dark green sheets of seaweed that are used to wrap sushi. These sheets are made in the same way as paper. Lavar seaweed is puréed and dried on racks in thin layers before being cut into sheets. Nori is often toasted over an open flame before use to bring out the salty oceanic flavors and to make it more pliable. It is almost always used in one of two ways: as a wrap for foods like sushi, or as a seasoning.

> Lightly wetting nori causes it to become tacky, helping it to stick to itself when rolled.

Nori-Seasoned Kale Chips

Potatoes may be the classic, but they're not the only vegetable in town that makes for a tasty chip. Kale chips have become all the rage in recent years, and for good reason. Kale is a true superfood packed with vitamins and minerals and even proven cancer-fighting properties. That, and they bake up to delightful crisp, just like the less healthy potato chips we all know and love. For this chip, nori acts as a seasoning, lending its toasty and lightly salty oceanic flavor to the pleasant "green" flavor of the kale. It's an unexpected flavoring for an equally unexpected chip.

6 to 8 large kale leaves
2 sheets of nori
2 tsp. olive oil
sprinkle of salt

Serves 2 to 4

1. Tear up nori sheets and pulse in a blender until only small flakes are left.
2. Tear kale leaves off of their stems in large pieces and place in a large bowl.
3. Drizzle over olive oil and use your hands to massage the oil into the kale until every surface of the leaves is coated.
4. Pour kale onto a large non-stick baking sheet and spread into a single even layer.
5. Sprinkle with up to 3 tbsp. of the nori flakes and a very light sprinkling of salt.
6. Bake at 350°F for 10 minutes.
7. Store any extra in an air-tight container at room temperature.

Spicy Tuna Temaki

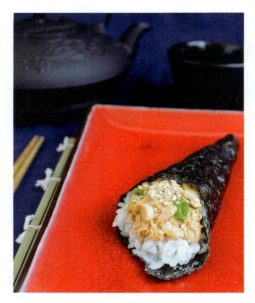

Here's another "casual sushi" that's simple enough to make ahead for popping in a lunch box yet still manages to be impressive as a party appetizer. Temaki means "handroll" and that's exactly how they're made, with rice and any number of tasty fillings rolled into a portable handheld cone. I've chosen a spicy tuna salad to fill these temaki sushi, but other great fillings include fresh shredded veggies with avocado, lemony sauteed shrimp, flaked salmon with wasabi, or nearly anything you have left over and need to use up.

Makes approx. 6

a 6 oz. can of tuna (packed in water)
1/4 cup mayo
1 tbsp. + 1 tsp. sriracha sauce
2 scallions (chopped)
1 tbsp. sesame seeds
5 sheets of nori (cut in half)
1 cup cooked short grain rice (pg.8)

1. Drain tuna and break up with a fork.
2. Add mayo, sriracha, chopped scallions, and sesame. Use fork to mix together.
3. Take a piece of nori with the rougher side facing upwards and place in front of you situated horizontally.
4. Place a heaping tablespoon of rice on the left side of the nori and spread out evenly to cover the left side, leaving the right side bare. Add a tablespoon of the tuna filling on top of the rice and spread out but not all the way to the edges.
5. Fold the bottom left corner over the filling and continue rolling towards the right.
6. Dab a little water on the hanging end of the nori so that it will stick to itself and seal the handroll.

Negi
Scallions

Also known as green onions or spring onions, the scallion is a young onion that has not yet grown a bulb. They are milder than bulb onions but stronger than chives, another variety of the onion family. These crisp green onions are a typical garnish for just about any Japanese dish. They are also used to flavor broths and add a spicy crunch to salads. Both the white and the green parts of the scallion are edible. The white has a crisper, spicier flavor, while the green is lighter and more grassy. Use one part or both depending on what flavor you wish to achieve.

> Grow scallions at home by placing a cut root end into a glass of water. As it grows, stand it upright and replace water as needed. You can do this over and over with the same root ends.

Negi Yakitori

Yakitori is Japanese bar food. You'll find it in any traditional izakaya, a Japanese bar that serves lots of small dishes that are meant to be washed down with copious amounts of beer. These skewers of vegetables, meat, or even organs are often cooked up right in front of you on a small indoor grill and served with a squeeze of lemon or a dollop of Japanese mayo. My favorite yakitori is definitely the negi, with large soft-centered slices of scallions squeezed between juicy bits of chicken, all glazed in a soy-based sauce and grilled to a slight char. Making this delicious izakaya staple at home is quick and simple, even if you don't have a grill of your own. I've developed this recipe to work with your ovens broiler setting, to recreate that delightfully charred surface without all the fuss of lighting up the grill, though if you simply love cooking outdoors you can absolutely use one. Mug of beer optional.

4 boneless and skinless chicken thighs
10-12 thick scallions
1 tbsp. soy sauce
1 tbsp. mirin
also needed: 8 to 10 bamboo skewers

Makes 8 to 10 skewers

1. Cut chicken thighs into small bite-sized pieces and marinate in the soy sauce and mirin for at least 20 minutes, or overnight.
2. Soak bamboo skewers in water for at least ten minutes prior to use.
3. Cut scallions into 1 inch pieces around the thickest part of the stalk.
4. Alternate piercing pieces of scallion and chicken on the soaked skewers and arrange on a foil-lined baking sheet.
5. Bake at 400°F for 10 minutes, then brush with more of the marinade and broil for 6 to 8 minutes on each side or until desired blackening. Protect your hands when rotating hot skewers.
6. Serve with a squeeze of lemon if desired.

Tempura Scallion Fritters

In a sukiyaki restaurant in Kyoto, I watched the chef rapidly chop an armload of scallions into an enormous pile of paper-thin rings. He mixed them with tempura batter and fried them up to make a crunchy little fried snack. Mere seconds in the hot oil rendered the hundreds of scallion bits sweet and soft, while the tempura that encased them crisped up to a golden crunch. They were sprinkled with a tiny bit of coarse salt while still hot and served with a light vinegar dipping sauce. It was one of the tastiest things I've ever eaten. I've tried to recreate those scallion tempura many times since then, and this recipe is the closest yet that I've come to the original. If there's one thing I've learned about how to make a good tempura, it's to start with very cold ingredients and keep the batter cold as you fry up each batch. These scallion fritters are an easy first foray into making tempura, and the best part is you get to eat your experiments.

Makes approx. 6

1/4 cup all-purpose flour
1/2 tsp. baking soda
1/2 cup panko breadcrumbs
1 cup thinly chopped scallions

1 small egg (still cold)
1/4 cup ice water
sprinkle of salt
vegetable or canola oil for frying

1. In a mixing bowl, whisk together flour and baking soda with a fork.
2. Add panko, scallions, egg, and ice water. Stir to combine and let rest in the refrigerator.
3. Add enough oil to a deep pan to come about 1/4 inch up the sides and bring up to medium high heat.
4. Drop 3 or 4 heaping spoonfuls of the batter into the hot oil and fry on each side for a minute to a minute and 15 seconds. Return batter to the refrigerator between batches.
5. Transfer fritters to a cooling rack with a paper towel underneath to collect excess oil. Sprinkle with salt while still hot.

Shiitake
Fragrant Mushroom

"Take" is the Japanese word for mushroom and "shii" refers to the type of tree it grows on. This is a common method of naming mushrooms in Japan. Used extensivelty in both dried and fresh forms, shiitake are often called "fragrant mushrooms" due to their earthy but sweet aroma. The dried form are often used to make a vegetarian version of dashi, due to the increased umami flavors created by the breakdown of proteins into amino acids that occurs during drying. Unlike some other mushroom stems, shiitake stems are rather woody and unpleasant to eat. Don't hesitate to cut them off and discard them. Like all mushrooms, shiitakes can produce Vitamin D when exposed to sunlight or UV light. Adding shiitakes and other mushrooms to your diet is a great way to make sure you're getting enough of this vital substance.

> To get the most mushroom for your money, look for shiitakes with larger caps than stems since you'll be throwing the stems away anyway.

Miso Shiitake Gravy

No kidding, I like this gravy more than any meat-based gravy I've ever had. The shiitake mushrooms do an excellent job of standing in for meat with their savory umami flavor, and the miso gives it a velvety richness and salty kick. Fresh aromatic rosemary completes this luscious vegetarian alternative that is good enough to be enjoyed by meat-eaters alike. In fact, the first time I made this gravy I used some leftover lamb drippings from a roast in lieu of the butter. I would highly encourage you to try it with the drippings from any cut of meat you choose if you love real homemade gravy as much as I do. But even without the drippings it's incredible over buttermilk biscuits, mashed potatoes, or your favorite roast.

2 cups finely chopped shiitake mushroom caps
2 cups vegetable stock
4 tbsp. butter (or meat drippings)
4 tbsp. all-purpose flour
2 tbsp. red or white miso paste
1 tbsp. soy sauce
1 tsp. apple cider vinegar
1 heaping tsp. finely chopped rosemary
1 tsp. black pepper
1 clove garlic (minced)

Serves 4 to 6

1. Saute shiitakes, garlic, and rosemary in butter until mushrooms are soft. Sprinkle flour over the mushrooms and stir until it forms a thick paste.
2. Add vegetable stock, soy sauce, apple cider vinegar, and black pepper and allow to come up to a simmer.
3. Add miso and whisk lightly to melt it into the warm gravy.
4. Serve over biscuits as shown or over anything you would enjoy with regular gravy.

GARLICKY SHIITAKE SAUTE

For me, there is no such thing as too much garlic, so these soft and springy shiitakes sauteed with seemingly tons of freshly minced garlic are just right. If you're not as keen on experiencing garlic overload, you can absolutely scale back the amount. And if shiitakes are an expensive item in your neck of the woods, feel free to supplement some of them with a more affordable mushroom, such as the crimini. Either way, they make a succulent side dish for any feast. I find them especially incredible spooned overtop a grilled flank steak, but they work equally well with warm soft tofu or even completely on their own.

10 oz. shiitake mushroom caps
3 large cloves of garlic (minced)
2 scallions (chopped)
1 tbsp. soy sauce
1 tbsp. mirin
2 tbsp. canola or sesame oil

Serves 2

1. Heat oil over medium heat in a non-stick pan. Add garlic and scallions and allow to soften.
2. Remove stems from mushrooms and slice any larger ones in half. Add to garlic and scallions.
3. Add soy and mirin and toss with tongs.
4. Cover with a lid for about 30 seconds to finish cooking the mushrooms with steam.

Edamame
Young Soy Beans

Edamame are immature soy beans harvested from the vine before fully ripened. They are most often found in the freezer section either whole, still in their fuzzy green pods, or shelled. The beans inside have a glossy sheen, bright springy green color, and subtly sweet flavor like many other young peas or beans. The pods themselves are not pleasant to eat, but split open easily to pop out the fresh edamame beans. Edamame are most often eaten as a snack food, boiled or steamed in their pods and served with a sprinkling of coarse salt. Though this is the most common preparation, they can be used in nearly any way you would use other beans or peas. Mash them up to make a dip, add them to soups and stews, or bake them up to a crispy crunch. They're a healthy alternative to chips or crackers and despite their "green vegetable" status, even children love them.

> Blanch shelled edamame in boiling water to enhance their bright green color and remove some of their starchiness.

Edamame and Avocado Crostini

If there's anything I love more than a crunchy snack, it's a creamy dip. Lemony chickpea hummus is a favorite, but I'm always looking for new and interesting dips for dunking crisp veggies and crackers. For this dip variation, the springy green flavor of edamame is blended with smooth avocado. It's delightful with seasonal crudités, but even better on a crunchy little piece of bite-sized toast. Squeeze a bit of lemon over each completed toast for a fresh and flavorful snack or impressive party appetizer.

Makes 8 to 10

1 cup frozen shelled edamame
1 small avocado
the juice from 1/4 of a lemon
1 large garlic clove
1 tsp. salt

10 cracks of freshly ground black pepper (1/4 tsp.)
2 tbsp. olive oil
1 small baguette or similar crusty bread
extra olive oil for drizzling

1. Slice baguette diagonally with a serrated knife into thin oval-shaped slices.
2. Arrange bread slices on a baking sheet and drizzle lightly with olive oil on both sides.
3. Toast bread under the broiler for a few minutes on each side, just until slices are lightly brown and crispy. Allow to cool on a cooling rack or towel.
4. Boil frozen edamame for 3 to 5 minutes and drain.
5. Add edamame, avocado, lemon juice, garlic, salt, pepper, and olive oil to a food processor and process until uniform in texture. You may need to stop and scrape down the sides of the mixing bowl with a spatula a few times to fully incorporate everything.
6. Spoon as much of the edamame and avocado mixture onto the slices as desired or serve separately as a dip for the crostini.

Crispy "Popcorn" Edamame

We all love crunchy snacks. For some it's crispy chips, for others it's crackers, and for still others only a bowl of buttery popcorn will do. But all that carb-laden junk food is just that – junk. It's hard to find a healthy snack that satisfies the craving for salt and fat without busting your gut. These crunchy roasted "popcorn" edamame come close. They have all the crispiness of a potato chip and are endlessly poppable, but contain just a scant teaspoon of oil. The delightful texture and bright flavor will have you snacking happy.

one 12oz. bag of frozen shelled edamame
1 tsp. olive oil
the juice from half a lemon (about 2 tsp.)
sprinkle of salt (to taste)

Makes approx. 2 cups

1. Allow edamame to thaw on the counter or under lukewarm running water.
2. In a large bowl, toss edamame with oil and lemon juice.
3. Bake at 375°F on a foil-lined baking sheet for 40 to 45 minutes or until lightly browned and crispy.
4. Sprinkle over salt to taste while the edamame are still hot. Allow to cool completely before storing in an airtight container.

Kabocha
Japanese Pumpkin

The kabocha is a medium-sized winter squash in about the same shape as a pumpkin, with dark green skin and bright orange flesh. The kabocha becomes sweet and creamy when cooked, making it an ideal ingredient for use in desserts, which is a favorite way to enjoy it in Japan. It's also excellent roasted, puréed for use in breads and cakes, or any way you enjoy other squashes. Don't throw out the seeds - like the seeds of most squashes, these are delicious when roasted and sprinkled with coarse salt.

> Hard winter squashes can be difficult to open. Use a smaller knife to cut in at the stem, wiggling the knife all the way down through the base. Repeat on other side and break in half.

KABOCHA CARBONARA

Pasta bathed in a luscious creamy sauce is one of the greatest gustatory joys, but all that goodness can be gut-busting. For this version of the classic carbonara, a dish typically composed of thin pasta in a sauce of parmesan and creamy raw egg, I've used a purée of roasted kabocha squash to enhance its luxurious texture. It lends an earthy but sweet flavor that pairs well with the salty parmesan and crisp bacon. Of course the squash makes it healthier, right? Not really. But at least you can say you managed to insert a serving of vegetables into this glorious carb fest.

1 small kabocha squash
4 oz. spaghetti or spaghettini pasta
4 slices bacon
2 eggs
1/2 cup freshly grated parmesan cheese
a heavy pinch of salt
freshly cracked black pepper to taste

Serves 4

1. Cut kabocha in half and scoop out the seeds. Cover lightly in oil and roast face down on a foil-lined baking sheet for 45 minutes at 400°F.
2. Allow kabocha to cool, then scoop the flesh out of the skin with a spoon and transfer to a food processor. Purée until smooth.
3. In a medium bowl, whisk together eggs, parmesan, 1/2 cup of the pureed kabocha, salt and pepper.
4. Chop bacon into small pieces and fry in a non-stick pan over medium heat until just crispy.
5. Boil noodles according to package directions, drain, and immediately add to the bacon.
6. Pour over egg and kabocha mixture and toss with tongs to combine. Plate immediately: the sauce will get too thick and the eggs overcooked if left in the hot pan.

Kabocha Nimono

"Nimono" are simmered dishes, usually made from starchy vegetables that will soak up whatever flavor is in the simmering liquid. You'll typically find nimono served as side dishes to the main course, or tucked into bento boxes for a healthy lunch. Kabocha is perfect for this method. The flesh takes on a soft baked potato-like texture and soaks up just enough sauce to add extra flavor without losing any of its own stand-out sweetness. It is customary to leave on a little bit of the skin for added fiber and a pop of color. Serve alongside your favorite roasted meat for a unique and simple side dish.

1 small to medium-sized kabocha squash
2 and 1/2 cups dashi (pg.7)
3 tbsp. soy sauce
2 tbsp. mirin
1 tbsp. sugar

Serves 4 to 6

1. Cut open kabocha and scrape out seeds. Use a knife to remove most of the green skin from the outside, leaving some for color. Cut into pieces of roughly the same size.
2. In a large saucepot, combine all other ingredients and add cut kabocha.
3. Bring up to a simmer over medium heat and cook uncovered for 15 to 20 minutes or until kabocha is tender.
4. Serve alone as a side dish or over rice.

Daikon
Japanese Radish

Daikon means "large root" in Japanese, and it can grow to be quite large - sometimes even as large as a grown man's arm. This member of the radish family has a much milder flavor than the small breakfast radishes common in the U.S. and is delicious in soups and stews where it absorbs the flavors of the other ingredients. It can be fantastic on its own though, steamed and topped with a salty miso sauce or as the common yellow pickle served with many Japanese dishes, called takuan, made by fermenting the roots in rice bran and vinegar for several months.

> Use daikon when it's very fresh as it can start to get rubbery and flexible as it ages, making it harder to peel and less desirable to eat.

Slow-Cooker Beef Shank and Daikon Stew

There is no other vegetable I've found that soaks up flavors while still maintaining its own unique character as well as daikon does. My absolute favorite application for daikon then, is in soups and stews. Long, slow cooking in a flavorful liquid renders it buttery-soft and full of juicy richness. Here, it takes the place of potatoes in this hearty stew of beef shanks and vegetables in a broth with Asian flavors. It retains its earthiness while soaking up the flavors of the salty soy broth and browned beef. You won't even miss the potatoes.

2 medium bone-in beef shanks (approx. 1.5 lbs. total)
10-12 slices of peeled daikon
1 large onion (cut into 8ths)
4 large carrots (chopped)
10-12 large shiitake mushroom caps
4 large garlic cloves (sliced thin)
1 bottle of brown or amber ale
3 cups dashi (pg.7)
1/4 cup soy sauce
1/4 cup red miso
2 tbsp. mirin
1 tbsp. canola oil

Serves 4 to 6

1. Fill the bottom of the slow cooker with the onion, daikon, carrots, shiitakes, and garlic.
2. Brown beef shanks on both sides in canola oil over medium high heat. Place over the vegetables in the slow cooker.
3. In a small saucepan - whisk together dashi, soy sauce, mirin, and miso over medium heat until miso is dissolved in the liquid.
4. Pour liquid over the beef shanks and vegetables, followed by the bottle of brown or amber ale. Cook on low for 9 hours.

Tempura Cod with Daikon Oroshi

Every time I've been served really good tempura, it's always come with a variety of dips and garnishes to eat it with. There's always a pretty little plate of colorful flavored salts, sour green ramp pickles, and always a side of daikon oroshi. This condiment is nothing more than finely grated daikon, awash in a bath of its own earthy juices. It is such an unexpectedly perfect compliment to any fried food, but especially so with fish, where it can mask some of the strong odors and flavors of oilier fishes. I like to serve it with cod, a white fish with an almost fluffy texture, lightly fried in a crust of golden tempura. Drizzled with a bit of dark soy, it is a match made in fried food heaven.

2 5oz. pieces of cod
1 large cold egg
3/4 cup flour
2/3 cup ice cold water
a 5-inch piece of peeled daikon
salt and soy sauce for seasoning
vegetable oil for frying

Serves 2

1. Dry cod pieces thoroughly with a paper towel, remove any pin bones, and salt all over.
2. Heat a half inch of vegetable oil in a pan to medium heat. Allow a full 5 minutes for oil to come up to temperature before using.
3. Lightly whisk together egg, ice water, and flour. Coat cod pieces in the batter and gently lower into the oil.
4. Allow cod to fry for 4 minutes on each side, then transfer to a drying rack.
5. Grate daikon using the star tip surface on a box grater or other very small grater that will reduce the daikon to a pulp.
6. Serve tempura cod topped with the daikon oroshi and drizzle lightly with soy sauce.

Satsuma-Imo
Japanese Sweet Potato

The reddish-purple skin and pale cream-colored flesh of the Japanese sweet potato may look very different from the orange variety more common in the West, but they do share a lot of similarities. This variety is also sweet, though the sweetness is more subtle and honeyed, and though it is a bit drier and starchier it still cooks up creamy and soft. It is excellent eaten in any way you would enjoy a regular sweet potato — baked whole or in wedges, boiled and mashed, or even fried. The Japanese really enjoy this as a dessert though, roasted over hot coals and eaten as is or mashed up to make a sweet filling for candies and pastries.

> The flesh of this type of potato will oxidize when exposed to the air. This will not affect the flavor, but a soak in water can stop them from browning if needed.

Sticky Baked Japanese Sweet Potato Fries

Who doesn't love french fries? Personally, the fry is my favorite way to enjoy potatoes, and the format tends to work with most starchy root vegetables. For these sweet potato fries, I tried to recreate another favorite Japanese snack called daigaku-imo. It's deep fried Japanese sweet potato sticks tossed in a sweet soy glaze. This version is baked rather than fried, and the glaze becomes caramelized and sticky in the hot oven making for a candy-like treat that's hard to stop eating.

1 large Japanese sweet potato
1 tbsp. soy sauce
1 tbsp. sugar
1 tbsp. mirin
1 tbsp. water
1 tsp. honey
canola or other flavorless oil to coat
sesame seeds to garnish (if desired)

Serves 2 to 4

1. Slice potatoes with skin on into medium sticks.
2. Mix together soy sauce, sugar, mirin, water, and honey in a small bowl. Microwave or heat in a small saucepan until sugar and honey are dissolved.
3. Toss potato sticks in oil and arrange on a foil-lined baking sheet.
4. Bake at 400°F for 45 minutes, flipping the fries over halfway through baking. In the last 15 minutes, brush on all of the soy mixture. It will turn into a sticky glaze by the end of baking.
5. While the fries are still hot, sprinkle with sesame seeds.

Japanese Sweet Potato Casserole

Undoubtedly, my favorite dish at Thanksgiving dinner is the sweet potato casserole. We always had the kind with a crunchy topping of brown sugar and pecans and it was sweet enough to stand in for dessert. In this version of that classic casserole I've tried to recreate the flavors of a traditional Japanese tea sweet, or wagashi, called the suito poteto. It consists of steamed and mashed sweet potato mixed with sugar, formed into a little ball, and baked with a glaze of egg yolk on top. I've done the same in this casserole, with a sweetened mash of Japanese sweet potatoes under a crisp browned crust of creamy yolk and sesame seeds. It's two classic dishes from two different cultures, combined for a unique and delicious result.

Serves 6 to 8

2 large Japanese sweet potatoes
1/4 cup sugar
1 tbsp. honey
3 tbsp. milk

4 tbsp. butter
2 egg yolks
pinch of salt
sesame seeds to garnish (if desired)

1. Peel sweet potatoes and cut into pieces of roughly the same size. Place in a pot filled 3/4 of the way with cold water and bring to a boil over high heat.
2. Boil for approximately 15 to 20 minutes or until potatoes are tender. Drain and transfer to a large mixing bowl.
3. Add butter, sugar, honey, and salt and mash until smooth. Wait until potatoes have cooled almost to room temperature before adding one of the egg yolks and mashing in.
4. Transfer mashed sweet potatoes to a 9x9 inch square baking dish. Use the back of a spoon to swirl grooves into the top of the potatoes then brush over the remaining egg yolk with a pastry brush and sprinkle over sesame seeds.
5. Bake at 350°F for 10 minutes to heat through, then broil for an additional 10 minutes or until golden brown on top.

Kuri
Chestnut

The chestnut tree belongs to the same family as oak and beech trees. The nuts this tree produces are valued all over the world for the pleasant texture, aroma, and flavor they develop when cooked, especially when roasted. Chestnuts are a seasonal treat in Japan and start to show up in almost everything in the fall. Some say the flavor is similar to that of a baked potato, subtly earthy but with a distinct nuttiness. The chestnut meat must first be extracted from the hard brown outer peel and from an inner peel called the pellicle. As with any nuts, the prize inside is well worth the work, but canned options exist if you don't feel like going to the trouble of roasting and peeling them yourself.

Cut an "X" into the bottom of each chestnut before roasting to allow steam pressure to release, otherwise they could explode!

KURI GOHAN

This is the one dish that nearly every Japanese family prepares when chestnut season rolls around. Roasted or boiled chestnuts are studded throughout the rice they cooked with, infusing it with a subtle sweetness and nuttiness throughout. The creamy texture of the chestnuts contrasts with the chewy rice for a luxurious mouthfeel. This is one of my very favorite gohan, a rice dish that is usually cooked with all of its ingredients mixed in beforehand.

12 to 15 chestnuts
1 cup uncooked short grain rice
2 tbsp. mirin
1 tbsp. soy sauce
1 and 1/2 cups dashi (pg.7)
2 tbsp. canola or vegetable oil

Serves 4 to 6

1. Soak chestnuts for 15 minutes in warm water. Carefully cut an "X" into each one with a paring knife and arrange cut side up on a baking sheet.
2. Roast chestnuts for 20 minutes at 350°F then transfer to a kitchen towel to cool. Peel chestnuts while they are still somewhat warm and discard any that are black or moldy.
3. In a large lidded pot, heat oil to medium heat. Add chestnuts and rice and toast for approximately one minute.
4. Add in mirin and soy sauce and stir to combine.
5. Pour in dashi and stir to lift any brown bits from the bottom of the pot. Turn heat up to high and allow to come to a boil.
6. As soon as the liquid starts to boil, turn the heat all the way down to the lowest setting, put the lid on, and set a timer for 15 minutes.
7. After 15 minutes, turn off the heat and allow to sit for an additional 10 minutes with the lid on. Fluff with a fork and serve.

CHESTNUT MINI-CHEESECAKES

One of the greatest things about the chestnut is that it is equally delicious in both savory and sweet preparations. The creamy texture of the chestnuts lends itself well to the smooth texture of cheesecake, and their subtle flavor nudges you to take bite after delicious bite, trying to taste more and more of it. Thankfully, the "mini" size of these cheesecakes is just right to satisfy your sweet tooth without going overboard. I've decided to use canned chestnut puree in this recipe to streamline the process. Roasting, peeling, and puréeing an armload of chestnuts needn't stand between you and these delectable little treats.

For the crust:
18 honey graham crackers (2 and 1/2 cups crushed)
1/4 cup sugar
1 stick melted butter
pinch of salt

For the filling:
2 8oz. blocks softened cream cheese
2/3 cup sugar
a 15.3 oz. can of unsweetened chestnut purée (1 and 3/4 cups)
3 eggs
1/8 tsp. vanilla
1/2 cup milk
pinch of salt   Makes 22 to 24

> For a single cake:
> Bake in a non-stick 9-inch springform pan at 325°F for 1 hour 30 min. to 1 hour 40 min. Let cool completely in pan before removing.

1. Pulse graham crackers, sugar, and salt in a food processor to make crumbs. Pour melted butter over the crumbs and pulse to combine.
2. Line two muffin pans with cupcake liners and fill each with 2 heaping tbsp. of the crust mixture. Tamp down with your fingers or the bottom of a glass.
3. Combine softened cream cheese and sugar in a mixer and mix for at least 1 minute or until fluffy. Add chestnut purée and mix completely.
4. Add eggs one at a time, mixing in between, then add remaining ingredients and beat on high until fluffy.
5. Fill each cupcake liner to just below the top. Bake at 315°F for 30 to 35 minutes. Allow to cool completely in pans before storing in refrigerator in an airtight container.
6. Serve cool and freeze any extras, which can be thawed overnight in the refrigerator when you are ready to eat.

Azuki
Sweet Red Bean

Believe it or not, these little red beans are most often eaten for dessert. Azuki beans are boiled with sugar and mashed to make a sweet creamy paste called an, or anko. This paste is used as a filling for sweet breads and cakes. It is usually sold canned and comes in a variety of textures from smooth and creamy to whole sweetened beans. Ocasionally red beans will show up in savory dishes. One of the more notable savory azuki bean dishes is sekihan, a simple dish of steamed short grain rice and azuki beans that is commonly eaten during celebration times. The beans infuse the rice with a festive red color - red sometimes symbolizing health or happiness in Japan.

> Normally you would want to rinse canned beans before using, but with red beans the sweet liquid is an important part of the product and should be used.

Sweetened Red Bean Paste

Anko is to the Japanese what chocolate is to the west. It's the quintessential dessert topping and filling that enhances almost any sweet. You can find a dense and smooth type of an, called koshi-an, in the center of bite-sized tea candies; a slightly chunkier version, called tsubushi-an, mixed into red bean ice cream or sandwiched between pancakes; and the whole beans mixed with sugar syrup, known as tsubu-an, that are often spooned over sundaes. It's a versatile confection that's easy to make and delicious on just about anything.

1 cup dried azuki beans
3 cups water
1 cup sugar
pinch salt

Makes about 3 cups

1. Bring the beans to a boil in enough water to cover, then immediately drain and rinse them.
2. Add par-boiled beans to a lidded pot and bring to a simmer with 3 cups of water.
3. Simmer covered for 45 minutes, stirring every 10 minutes and adding more water if the beans start to dry out and stick to the bottom of the pot.
4. When beans are done, stir in sugar and allow to dissolve completely.
5. Store in an air-tight container in the refrigerator for several weeks or in the freezer for up to 6 months.

Dorayaki

One of my favorite ways to enjoy anko is in a dorayaki. These mini pancake sandwiches are portable, not too sweet, and just the right size. They're a great afternoon snack or healthy dessert option, and even work well as a breakfast pastry. In fact, I would encourage you to top your next stack of fluffy golden pancakes with a dollop of sweet anko, fresh berries, and even a little whipped cream in lieu of the usual hot butter and maple syrup. You won't regret it.

2 eggs
1/2 cup sugar
1 tbsp. honey
1/3 cup water
1/2 tsp. baking soda
1 cup all-purpose flour
approx. 3/4 cup sweetened red bean paste (previous pg.)

Makes 8

1. In a mixing bowl, whisk together eggs, sugar, and honey.
2. In a separate bowl, stir to dissolve baking soda in water. Add to eggs and sugar.
3. Add flour a little at a time mixing well between each addition.
4. Heat a large non-stick pan to medium-low heat and spray with a flavorless oil such as canola.
5. Use 2 tbsp. of batter for each pancake. Cook on the first side for approximately 3 to 4 minutes or until the bottoms are golden brown. Flip over and cook for an additional minute. Transfer to a cooling rack or kitchen towel to cool.
6. Spread one pancake with anko paste and place another on top to create the dorayaki sandwich.

Nashi
Asian Pear

The nashi, sometimes called an asian pear or shinko pear, has the subtle sweetness of a pear mixed with the crunch and crispness of an apple. They range in color anywhere from a bright golden yellow to a rich clay brown and are speckled all over with light-colored spots. These fruits are most often eaten out of hand as a snack or healthy dessert, but they can be used in any way you would normally enjoy an apple or pear, such as baked into desserts, or simply sliced up over a salad. They don't hold up very well to poaching though, as it tends to leach out the subtle flavor. Look for them in the fall when other pears and apples start to make their first appearances on store shelves.

> Choose a nashi that is firm and smooth with no traces of green. They're often harvested under-ripe and will need to soften up on the counter for as long as two weeks before eating.

Nashi Pear Sauce

The first time I made applesauce from scratch I was floored. Not only was it incredibly easy, but the results tasted so much better than any store-bought sauce, many of which are loaded with corn syrup and preservatives. Nashis work wonderfully as a stand-in for apples in this luscious fruit sauce. They hold their shape well when cooked and retain their texture even after being puréed. The mild flavor of the pears is paired with a floral orange blossom honey and is lightly spiced with nutmeg and ginger. It's equally delicious whether dolloped over yogurt, ice cream, or even pork chops. My favorite way to eat it is right out of the spoon.

3 large nashi asian pears
2 tsp. orange blossom honey (or other honey)
1 tsp. white sugar
1/2 tsp. ground nutmeg
1/2 tsp. ground ginger
zest of half a lemon
a tiny pinch of salt

Makes approx. 2 cups

1. Peel, core, and chop asian pears into chunks.
2. In a bowl, combine pears with other ingredients and stir to coat.
3. Bake in a small baking dish at 375°F for 1 hour.
4. Pulse baked pears and juices in a food processor to desired consistency.
5. Store in a sealed container in the refrigerator for up to 2 weeks. Freeze any extra for up to 6 months.

ASIAN PEAR AND GINGER CRUMBLE

My favorite desserts are always the ones with warm roasted fruit contrasted against something creamy and cool. I can never get enough hot apple crumble in the fall, topped with swiftly melting vanilla ice cream. This asian pear and ginger crumble has all the elements of a comforting baked dessert. With the floral, almost rose-like flavor of the mellow asian pears pairing with mildly spicy fresh ginger, it's an exotic spin on the classic formula. Pair this with coconut ice cream, or the old standard vanilla, for a cool-weather treat.

Serves approx. 6

For the filling:
2 asian pears
1 tbsp. sugar
3/4 tsp. fresh grated ginger root
1/2 tsp. cinnamon

For the crumble topping :
1/2 cup all-purpose flour
3 tbsp. sugar
1/4 tsp. salt
1/4 tsp. cinnamon
4 tbsp. softened butter

1. Peel, core, and chop asian pears into similarly-sized pieces. Toss with sugar, ginger, and cinnamon in a bowl, then pour into a baking dish.
2. In a separate bowl, combine all crumble topping ingredients and mash together with the back of a fork or with your hands until it looks crumbly.
3. Pour crumble topping over fruit and bake at 350°F for 50 minutes.
4. Serve warm alone or with ice cream.

Kaki
Persimmon

The persimmon is a much underappreciated fruit. This is largely because persimmons, both the large acorn-shaped Hachiya variety and the smaller Fuyu, are sold while they are still hard and unripe. Many people who think they hate persimmons have only been exposed to eating these underripened ones, which can be very astringent and leave an unpleasant film in the mouth. While the Fuyus can be eaten while still crisp, it is best to allow the Hachiya variety to ripen to the point of looking wrinkled and fall-apart soft. At this stage, they have a very pleasant flavor similar to mango or apricot, but with the texture of jam or preserves. The Fuyus are similar in flavor but with a subtle starchiness reminiscent of winter squashes and a texture somewhere between a tomato and a nectarine. Both varieties can be enjoyed alone but also work very well baked into breads and pastries.

> Ripe Hachiya persimmon can be used 1 to 1 in place of applesauce, mashed banana, or pumpkin in any recipe that calls for these ingredients.

Persimmon Walnut Breakfast Bread

The texture of this bread reminds me of the perfect banana bread - soft, moist, and pulls apart into poppable bites. A luscious layer of persimmon runs through its center and bits of walnuts are studded throughout. This is a wonderful way to enjoy Hachiya persimmons as their soft overripe flesh is perfect for adding moisture and flavor to baked goods. This bread is not too sweet and can be enjoyed at any time. I like to pop a thick slice in the toaster oven and eat it warm with a thin layer of melted butter for breakfast.

1/4 cup softened butter
1/2 cup packed brown sugar
1/4 cup white sugar, plus extra for sprinkling
1 1/2 cups all-purpose flour
1 1/2 tsp. baking powder
1 tsp. baking soda
1 and 1/2 tsp. cinnamon
1/2 tsp. nutmeg
1/4 tsp. salt
1/4 cup milk
3/4 cup crushed walnuts
the flesh of 2 very ripe Hachiya persimmons

Makes approx. 10 to 12 servings

1. Cream together butter and sugars in a stand mixer. Add one cup of the persimmon flesh and mix through.
2. In a separate bowl, whisk together dry ingredients then add to the wet mix in three additions, mixing between each addition. Fold in walnuts with a spatula.
3. Add half the batter to a buttered and floured loaf pan. Add any remaining persimmon flesh in a line down the center and top with the other half of the batter, spreading evenly.
4. Sprinkle with white sugar and bake in a preheated 350°F oven for approximately 1 hour.
5. Let cool in loaf pan for 15 minutes then turn out and finish cooling on a wire rack. Store in an air-tight container in the refrigerator for up to a week.

Persimmon Salsa with Cinnamon Chips

Persimmons may be a fall fruit, but the crisp Fuyus lend themselves especially well to more summery preparations. They can be sliced over a salad of tender spring greens, blended with peaches or mangoes for a sweet summer smoothie, or diced into a fresh fruit salsa to serve over grilled fish. This sweet and citrusy dessert-style fruit salsa of finely chopped Fuyu persimmons in cool yogurt is a fresh warm weather treat that gets scooped up with crispy homemade cinnamon sugar tortilla chips. Refreshing fruit salads don't have to end with summer when an abundance of juicy fall persimmons can be found.

For the salsa:
2 Fuyu persimmons
1 heaping tbsp. plain yogurt
1/2 tsp. sugar
zest and juice of 1 clementine or small orange
a pinch of cinnamon

For the chips :
4 medium flour tortillas
1 tbsp. melted butter
cinnamon and sugar for sprinkling

Serves 4 to 6

1. Peel persimmons by slicing off the top and bottom, then slicing down the sides. Cut the flesh away from the firmer center part and mince into very small pieces.
2. In a small bowl, combine the minced persimmon with the yogurt, sugar, cinnamon, zest, and juice. Stir to combine.
3. For the chips, brush tortillas liberally with butter on one side and sprinkle with desired amount of cinnamon and sugar.
4. Bake tortillas on a baking sheet at 350°F for 15 to 20 minutes. You may need to pop air bubbles in the tortillas with a knife as they begin to fill with steam in order to keep the chips relatively flat.

Matcha
Green Tea Powder

There is enough knowledge on the subject of tea to fill an entire book on its own. Almost all tea varieties, with the exception of rooibos, yerba mate, and herbal teas, come from the same Camellia Sinensis plant and differ only in how they are processed after harvest. Matcha is a finely ground powder made from only the youngest shade-grown tea leaves. It is used in Japanese tea ceremonies where it is frothed with hot water using a special bamboo whisk called a chasen, and served in a wide bowl called a chawan. It is often savored alongside a type of small dessert, called a wagashi, and is used as a flavoring for these types of sweets as well. It is high in powerful antioxidants and vitamins, and contains L-theanine, a naturally-occuring amino acid that has been shown to increase alertness and mental acuity without the jittery effects often associated with coffee.

Matcha is highly prone to oxidation, which will render it dull in color and flavor. Keep in a tightly sealed container stored away from direct light and use within 6 months.

GREEN TEA AND PISTACHIO SEMIFREDDO

Fine matcha green tea is undoubtedly a luxury item, and for good reason with all the care and attention that goes into making it. I often choose to buy a lower quality matcha when I'm only intending to use it for baking to lower the cost, but this time I thought I'd go all out and use the good stuff to make an over-the-top luxury dessert. This light-as-air semifreddo is studded throughout with another green luxury item - pistachios. Both the pistachios and the matcha have that slightly bitter "green" flavor that I've balanced with the tartness of yogurt and a drizzle of sweet good-quality honey. It's a truly elegant, albeit pricey dessert which will easily serve 12 lucky dinner guests, but the recipe can be easily halved if you'd just like to keep an extra special treat for yourself waiting in the freezer.

Serves 10 to 12

1 pint heavy whipping cream
1 cup plain yogurt
1/2 cup sugar
2 tbsp. matcha powder

pinch salt
1 cup chopped pistachios
a good-quality honey to garnish (if desired)

1. With a hand mixer or stand mixer, whip the heavy cream, sugar, salt, and matcha powder vigorously until stiff peaks are formed.
2. Gently fold in yogurt and pistachios with a spatula.
3. Transfer mixture into a parchment paper lined loaf pan or other dish and cover. Freeze for at least 4 hours.
4. Before serving, allow to sit at room temperature for 15 to 20 minutes before inverting onto a serving dish. Drizzle with honey and slice to serve.
5. This dessert is very prone to freezer burn. Keep it wrapped in wax paper or parchment and sealed in a plastic container to protect it.

MATCHA MUFFINS

I've never been much of a coffee person, but I just can't start my day without a cup of tea, or two, or three... It's no surprise then that I'm all too eager to inject even more of the good stuff into my breakfast as well. These matcha muffins may not have enough caffeine to perk you up, but they will certainly fill you up as the subtle green tea flavor will leave you unable to stop at just one. I like to use a less expensive matcha intended specifically for baking so as not to break the bank before breakfast. If you really want to get fancy though, add a dollop of sweetened red bean paste (pg.86) into each muffin before baking for an authentic Japanese treat.

1 and 1/2 cups all-purpose flour
2 tbsp. matcha powder
1 and 1/2 tsp. baking powder
1/2 tsp. baking soda
pinch of salt

1/2 cup sugar
6 tbsp. melted unsalted butter
6 tbsp. milk
1 large egg
1/2 cup plain yogurt

Makes approx. 12

1. In a large bowl, combine flour, matcha, baking powder, baking soda, and salt and whisk together thoroughly.
2. In a separate bowl, whisk together sugar and melted butter. Whisk in egg, then milk and yogurt.
3. Add wet mixture to dry and gently stir just until there is no visible dry mix showing. Allow to rest for about 5 minutes to allow the dry ingredients to fully absorb the wet.
4. Spray a standard muffin pan with non-stick spray and spoon the muffin mixture in to approximately 3/4 of the way up the sides.
5. Bake at 375°F for 20 minutes. Allow muffins to cool in the pan just until you can get them out safely, then transfer to a cooling rack.
6. Store in an air-tight container at room temperature for up to 4 days. Reheat in a toaster oven for a better texture than the microwave provides.

いただきます

Itadakimasu

"Let's eat!"

About the Author

I'm Alayna Tucker, author of the blog Thyme Bombe, where I write about the foods I love to eat and the recipes they've inspired. I live in Decatur, GA with my husband Jeff and our two neurotic cats.

My love for Japanese food started as a teenager with my interest in the colorful culture of Japan. As a young adult learning how to cook for the first time, I wanted to experience the flavors of Japan for myself and sought to learn how to recreate them in my own kitchen. As I became a more accomplished and confident cook, my knowledge of Japanese cooking grew to become the style I now feel most comfortable cooking in.

While I may not be an expert in every aspect of traditional Japanese cooking, I feel confident in my mastery of Japanese ingredients as I've found more and more ways to incorporate them into the foods I love. My hope is that this book will expose you to some new and exciting flavors, and give you the confidence to try them in your own kitchen.

For more Japanese-inspired recipes like the ones found in this book, as well as recipes from cuisines around the world, visit my blog Thyme Bombe at http://thymebombe.com/ You can also email me at alayna@thymebombe.com with any questions or comments.

INDEX

A

Anko 86
Asian Pear 88
   Asian Pear and Ginger Crumble 90
   Nashi Pear Sauce 89
Author Info 99
Azuki 85
   Dorayaki 87
   Sweetened Red Bean Paste 86

B

Basics 5
   Dashi 7
   Stovetop Sushi Rice 8
   Sushi-Su 9
Bread 92
Buckwheat Noodles 48
   Caramelized Onion Soba 49
   Chilled Zaru-soba with Mentsuyu Dipping Sauce 50

C

Carbonara 71
Cheesecake 84
Chestnut 81
   Chestnut Mini-Cheesecakes 84
   Kuri Gohan 82
Crostini 67
Crumble 90

D

Daikon 73
   Slow-Cooker Beef Shank and Daikon Stew 74
   Tempura Cod with Daikon Oroshi 76
Dashi 7

E

Edamame 66
   Crispy "Popcorn" Edamame 68
   Edamame and Avocado Crostini 67

F

Fermented Rice Alcohol 28
   Sake Risotto with Seared Scallops 30
   Sake-Steamed Mussels 29
Fermented Soy Bean Paste 18
   Miso-Glazed Salmon 19
   Miso Soup 21
Fragrant Mushroom 62
   Garlicky Shiitake Saute 64
   Miso Shiitake Gravy 63
Fried Instant Noodles 45
   Black Pepper Chicken Ramen 47
   Sesame Broth Ramen with Bacon 46
Fritters 61
Fuyu 91

G

Gohan 82
Goma 38
   Sesame Kara-Age 39
   Toasted Sesame Blondies 40
Grapefruit 26
Gravy 63
Green Tea 94
Green Tea Powder 94
   Green Tea and Pistachio Semifreddo 95
   Matcha Muffins 97

H

Hachiya 91

I

Ingredients 11
   Azuki 85
   Daikon 73
   Edamame 66
   Goma 38
   Kabocha 70
   Kaki 91
   Komezu 25
   Kuri 81
   Matcha 94
   Mirin 22

Miso 18
Nashi 88
Negi 59
Nori 55
Panko 41
Ramen 45
Sake 28
Satsuma-Imo 77
Shiitake 62
Shoyu 15
Soba 48
Sushi Kome 12
Tofu 35
Udon 52
Wasabi 31
Introduction 1

J

Japanese Bread Crumbs 41
   Korokke 42
   Tonkatsu 44
Japanese Horseradish 31
   Creamy Wasabi Potato Salad 34
   Wasabi Party Cheese Ball 33
Japanese Pumpkin 70
   Kabocha Carbonara 71
   Kabocha Nimono 72
Japanese Radish 73
   Slow-Cooker Beef Shank and Daikon Stew 74
   Tempura Cod with Daikon Oroshi 76
Japanese Sweet Potato 77
   Japanese Sweet Potato Casserole 80
   Sticky Baked Japanese Sweet Potato Fries 79

K

Kabocha 70
   Kabocha Carbonara 71
   Kabocha Nimono 72
Kaki 91
   Persimmon Salsa with Cinnamon Chips 93
   Persimmon Walnut Breakfast Bread 92
Kale Chips 57

Komezu 25
    Mango Salad with Grapefruit Ginger
        Vinaigrette 26
    Spicy Cucumber Quick Pickles 27
Kuri 81
    Chestnut Mini-Cheesecakes 84
    Kuri Gohan 82

M

Matcha 94
    Green Tea and Pistachio Semifreddo
        95
    Matcha Muffins 97
Mentsuyu 50
Mirin 22
    Mirin-Glazed Roasted Carrots 23
    Sweet Cotton Omelet 24
Miso 18
    Miso-Glazed Salmon 19
    Miso Soup 21
Muffins 97
Mussels 29

N

Nashi 88
    Asian Pear and Ginger Crumble 90
    Nashi Pear Sauce 89
Negi 59
    Negi Yakitori 60
    Tempura Scallion Fritters 61
Nimono 72
Nori 55
    Nori-Seasoned Kale Chips 57
    Spicy Tuna Temaki 58

O

Okayu 14
Omelet 24
Oroshi 76

P

Panko 41
    Korokke 42
    Tonkatsu 44
Persimmon 91
    Persimmon Salsa with Cinnamon Chips
        93
    Persimmon Walnut Breakfast Bread 92

Pickles 27
Pistachio 95

R

Ramen 45
    Black Pepper Chicken Ramen 47
    Sesame Broth Ramen with Bacon 46
Rice Vinegar 25
    Mango Salad with Grapefruit Ginger
        Vinaigrette 26
    Spicy Cucumber Quick Pickles 27
Risotto 30

S

Sake 28
    Sake Risotto with Seared Scallops 30
    Sake-Steamed Mussels 29
Salsa 93
Satsuma-Imo 77
    Japanese Sweet Potato Casserole 80
    Sticky Baked Japanese Sweet Potato
        Fries 79
Scallions 59
    Negi Yakitori 60
    Tempura Scallion Fritters 61
Scallops 30
Seaweed Paper 55
    Nori-Seasoned Kale Chips 57
    Spicy Tuna Temaki 58
Semifreddo 95
Sesame Seeds 38
    Sesame Kara-Age 39
    Toasted Sesame Blondies 40
Shiitake 62
    Garlicky Shiitake Saute 64
    Miso Shiitake Gravy 63
Short Grain Rice 12
    Chicken Okayu 14
    Smoked Salmon Temari-zushi 13
Shoyu 15
    Honey-Soy Roast Beef Shoulder 17
    Shoyu Tamago 16
Soba 48
    Caramelized Onion Soba 49
    Chilled Zaru-soba with Mentsuyu Dip-
        ping Sauce 50
Soy Bean Curd 35
    Hiyayakko 36
    Tahini-Miso Baked Tofu 37

Soy Sauce 15
    Honey-Soy Roast Beef Shoulder 17
    Shoyu Tamago 16
Stovetop Sushi Rice 8
Sushi Kome 12
    Chicken Okayu 14
    Smoked Salmon Temari-zushi 13
Sushi-Su 9
Sweet Red Bean 85
    Dorayaki 87
    Sweetened Red Bean Paste 86
Sweet Rice Seasoning 22
    Mirin-Glazed Roasted Carrots 23
    Sweet Cotton Omelet 24

T

Tamago 16
Temaki 58
Temari-zushi 13
Thick Wheat Noodles 52
    Tsukimi Udon 53
    Yaki-Udon 54
Tofu 35
    Hiyayakko 36
    Tahini-Miso Baked Tofu 37

U

Udon 52
    Tsukimi Udon 53
    Yaki-Udon 54

W

Wasabi 31
    Creamy Wasabi Potato Salad 34
    Wasabi Party Cheese Ball 33

Y

Yakitori 60
Young Soy Beans 66
    Crispy "Popcorn" Edamame 68
    Edamame and Avocado Crostini 67

Z

Zaru-soba 50

Printed in Great Britain
by Amazon.co.uk, Ltd.,
Marston Gate.